T0270245

THE END *of* TENNESSEE

THE END *of* TENNESSEE

A Memoir

RACHEL M. HANSON

THE UNIVERSITY OF
SOUTH CAROLINA PRESS

© 2024 Rachel M. Hanson

All rights reserved.

Published by the University of South Carolina Press
Columbia, South Carolina 29208

uscpress.com

Printed in the United States of America

Library of Congress Cataloging-in-Publication Data
can be found at https://lccn.loc.gov/2024012312

ISBN: 978-1-64336-493-3 (paperback)
ISBN: 978-1-64336-494-0 (ebook)

This memoir reflects the author's present recollections of experiences over time. Some names have been changed, some events have been compressed, and some dialogue has been recreated.

For my little brothers and sister

CONTENTS

On Seventeen in Appalachia

Not a year before I ran away from home at seventeen, I stepped out of the house at dusk, still able to see shrub oaks thinned out for winter, fame flower, too, and dun clay so wet the smell of it seemed settled in my skin. At my back, pastures spread far, darkened where dairy cows huddled for warmth in a slow January drizzle. I crossed the road, walked the length of my neighbor's yard, and knocked on his door, asking to play the piano he'd mentioned I was welcome to weeks earlier. I'd played when I was younger, when one of the houses we rented had an upright in the living room. Here, at my neighbor's, I hoped to remember how to make the keys work, and for the briefest moment, have some space to be more than a second mother to my siblings. Earlier in the day while I was taking out the trash, my neighbor had called out to me to feel free to come over and take a break when I found time to slip away. He said he was sad to see someone as young as myself so work-worn and had let me practice at his piano several times before.

It wasn't until I was sitting on the piano bench that I noticed, when my neighbor pointed it out, how my hair fell more than halfway down my back. I looked down at the frayed ends and couldn't recall the last time it'd been trimmed. He touched it, said it was soft, lovely untethered. I gave an uneasy smile, told myself he didn't mean to leave his hands there so long. I'd hoped to speak to anyone who wouldn't ask me for a thing, though I see now there was a question in his fingertips.

It didn't take long for him to show me the crack he kept hidden inside a pot on top of the refrigerator. He let me hold it—the small milky colored rocks kept in a baggie, told me how it must be boiled, made liquid in a spoon. I did not show my surprise, handled the drugs and the information as if it were no big deal. Because I was never sure what was normal and what was not, I'd been trying to learn how to keep a straight face when I wasn't sure how to react to a situation. Still, I looked across the way, back to where my little siblings lay sleeping under the covers I'd tucked them into. My instinct told me to move toward them, so I did, slowly, as if that had been my plan all along, before I held the drugs. But on the front porch steps my neighbor stopped me and pressed a small bottle of gold schnapps in my hand: "A girl should have a present on her birthday."

I didn't go back inside our house immediately but walked around to the back yard and sat beneath the largest of two oak trees, its limbs stretched too far over the tin roof of the house, and reached long across the barbed wire fence that separated our property from the farmer's next door. There was something about the cold, that low whispering wind, that told me I would not last in Tennessee much longer, and the knowledge of it made me desperate to find a way to stay, a way that already I knew did not exist.

Later, inside our house, I shared the booze with my older brother, Ben, at the kitchen table, both of us wondering if the gold was real. We said, "here's to us," drank fast, the cinnamon burn stretching grins on our faces, freezing there when our mother rang from the psychiatric ward of the hospital, a ward she'd seen more than once after insisting she had a physical illness that did not exist. She offered me a belabored breath then said, "I guess I should be saying happy birthday." I hated her for it—that sigh. I passed the phone to my brother, took scissors to the bathroom—cut my hair.

In the morning, after I fed and dressed my five younger siblings, we sat huddled together in the living room watching cartoons. I looked at each one of their faces as they smiled and laughed at the television. I told myself I could not leave them, to look harder for a way to stay.

Talking in Tongues

In nearly every house my family ever lives in, starting with the first one I remember, when I was four years old, my father makes improvements, or what he thinks are improvements. His jobs are rarely completed, but he continues to take them on with a strange amount of pleasure. He tears down walls or works on the landscape, and in the Texas house, he rips out the storm cellar, leaving behind an aftermath of broken ground, large and small pieces of concrete, and busted two-by-fours with rusty nails jutting in all directions that will eventually pierce through Ben's foot when we play tag.

A chain-link fence divides our yard from the neighbor's, but it doesn't hinder the three of us kids from sneaking into their yard to play on their swing set when their father, Brett, isn't home. I have watched him yell at his dog, Dundee, which only aggravates the shaggy, cream-colored mutt and motivates him to add a low growl between his barks. Brett yells his threats at the dog until his voice cracks and goes hoarse. Then he attempts to beat Dundee but usually fails as Dundee is too quick and nearly always manages to escape to a hole underneath the house. On occasion a random object in the yard, a stick, a baseball, or a child's toy, finds its way into Brett's hands. He flails the object toward Dundee as he runs for his hiding place, and once in a while the object manages to make a thwacking sound against the poor dog's body. Once Dundee escapes, Brett stands a few feet from the hole and speaks to the dog in tongues.

I ask my mother why Brett talks that way to Dundee, and she tells me it's because he's a preacher, and that's how preachers and other people filled with the spirit speak. She says Brett is faking, that the spirit doesn't live inside him. I ask her if the spirit lives inside her and whether she talks in tongues. She says she does, but only when the spirit chooses to move within her.

Eventually Dundee disappears altogether. I imagine Brett has finally carried out one of his many threats, and I contemplate which one Brett chose. I decide on the threat that entails Brett dropping Dundee off a bridge with rocks tied around his neck. Maybe Dundee gets the chance to sink his teeth deep into the skin of his captor. I hope he draws blood. Something tells me Dundee will sink, but I ignore that thought, instead choosing to believe he manages to slip away from his rock anchor, come up for air, and then swim to a dusty shore. Maybe a nice woman in the country will find him and feed him chicken-fried steak leftovers.

Sometimes Brett rips switches from trees in his yard to use on his two children, Josie and James. Josie is seven years old, a year older than Ben and two years older than me. James and I are practically the same age. Both Josie and James always want to play outside with us, maybe because they aren't allowed to very often. They don't spend the day outdoors like me and my brothers do when we stay with our parents. James says it's because his mother is afraid they will get sunburned. Every once in a while, Josie sneaks into the yard, she plays hide and sneak, and in our hiding place she pulls down her pants and tells me about what goes between her legs. She knows all about privates, she tells me, because there have been things in her before. I feel weird when she does this but understand it's a secret and so keep her displays and unwanted information to myself.

Most days I spend hours playing by a tree stump. I like to trace the cracks and circles in the wood, to feel the strange, smooth inner remains of a tree. Today, I hum, imagine it's a table set with food and wonder what time our mother will let me go inside to eat because I'm especially hungry. Even Ben has made his way over to the stump, leans against its base and says, "I'm starving."

When our mother finally allows the three of us kids back in the house, it's for food. Seth, who constantly reminds me and Ben that, at eight years old, he is the most in charge, is the one who almost always makes the sandwiches. But today is unusual, and both my parents are home. They stand in the kitchen; a loaf of bread, bologna, mustard, Miracle Whip, pickled okra, and cheese wrapped in clear plastic wrappers are all spread out in front of them on the countertop. I lie on the living room floor and sing about how hungry I am. My mother watches from the kitchen, and so does my father. They smile at me and ask if I want Miracle Whip or mustard on my sandwich. I'm surprised by the question. Seth never asks. He knows how Ben likes mustard and I like Miracle Whip. I tell my parents what I want and hurry to the table and wait for the food.

After eating, I go back outside to my stump, and shortly after Ben follows. Mustard has stained the corner of his mouth a muted yellow. Over his shoulder he carries a golf club that our father sawed down, wrapped in tape, and gave him. He carries it casual-like, as if to say no one else in the world could ever carry a golf club the way he does.

"Rachel, you need to move. I'm practicing my golf swing."

"No, I was here first, besides I'm in the middle of a game."

"Well, I'm telling you, I have to practice my swing and you need to move."

"I'm not moving, Ben. I was here first."

"If you don't move you might get hit."

"Well, I'm not moving."

"Okay, don't say I didn't warn you."

He walks in front of me, and I try to ignore him, but his exaggerated arm stretches and hip swings are funny. He glances over his shoulder and I laugh at him, and then look back at my stump, which I've imagined into a playground for small animals and insects that talk to each other.

"Last warning, Rachel!"

I ignore him. A second later I'm on my back, staring up at a clear sky through clots of dirt and blood. Ben blocks out the sunlight when he leans over my body, he lets the golf club fall to the ground where it lands with a light thud, and then he lets out a yell and runs inside. I get up, walk to the back porch and lean against the concrete steps with an extended arm, chin resting on my chest as I watch drops of blood fall to the ground, darkening the dirt. Ben comes running out of the back door.

"Mom doesn't believe me. I told her you were hurt, but she doesn't believe me. She won't get off the phone!" Ben says.

"Get Seth," I tell him.

Ben finds Seth, who had been dribbling his basketball in the driveway. Me and Ben had given up trying to dribble the ball. It always fell sadly with a dull, lifeless thump, never bouncing back high enough. Seth said it was because we didn't put enough energy into it, and that we had to smack the ball harder if it was to bounce back up from the dirt.

"Rachie, you're hurt bad," Seth says. "I'll go get Dad."

Our father is in the front yard, smoking his pipe and mowing the grass he planted and managed to grow the year before. By the time he gets to me, I'm sitting against one of the four posts that hold up the back porch, hand on my forehead, feeling the blood seep through my fingers and drip warmly down my face and then get sticky on my palms. My father puts a handkerchief on my head, tells me to hold it there and then runs inside. He returns with a washcloth, picks me up, and tiny pieces of grass fall off his overalls onto my clothes.

"We're going to the hospital."

"No, I don't want to go."

"You have to go." My mother's voice is clear, breaking through the blood and the pain and the confusion. I hear her footsteps up ahead—she is going to the car. My father carries me like an infant, places me in my mother's arms in the front seat. At the hospital they give me a shot, stitches, and then a sticker of a bear dressed up as a doctor. I keep that sticker long after the adhesive has given into the dirt that coats it and the color of the bear has all but faded away.

Back at home, my father gives me grape-flavored Tylenol, and Ben watches, then tells me he's sorry, and I can tell from his splotchy skin he's been crying. I know Ben likes the Tylenol, so I hide one of the three I've been given.

"I didn't think it was long enough to reach you, Rachie. I wouldn't have swung it if I thought it would have really hit you."

"It's okay, it doesn't even hurt now," I say, and give him the Tylenol.

"Are you sure?" he asks, looking at the Tylenol hungrily.

"Yep."

He crunches the Tylenol between his teeth and then lets the broken pieces melt on his tongue.

A few days later our mother leaves us with Addie, Brett's wife. Addie feeds everyone apples and lets me play inside their cool air-conditioned house. But when Brett comes home he puts all of us to bed on pallets in the den. He says it is naptime. Instead of taking a nap the five of us whisper and giggle, which provokes Brett, who stands like a giant as he glares, warns that he will beat the next person that says a word. I'm terrified of Brett and lay quiet, but James doesn't listen. He isn't tired, and it doesn't take long for him to crawl over to my pallet out of boredom.

"Move your bangs," he whispers, "I want to see your stitches."

I don't say a word or make an effort to fulfill his request. Instead I just stare at him, his white-blond hair is long, fine, and very straight. It almost touches my forehead when he leans over my face, and I notice how small his hands are as he pushes the bangs away from my hurt with one hand and with the other gently touches the stitches.

"Yep, you gotta a lot of stitches. Good thing you didn't die," he whispers.

His cool fingers handle my hair gently and they feel good on my forehead. I smile at him, and he smiles back. Both of us giggle, and little snickers sneak up our throats and escape through our noses. Then Brett is back, hovering over the both of us. By the look on my face, James knows Brett is there; he freezes, poised like a statue on his knees, peering into my stiff face. Brett grabs him by the ribcage, jerks him into the air, almost drops him, but catches him by a wrist. James swings in the air and nothing more than a gasp for breath escapes him. Brett starts to hit him, thuds land on the back of James's legs, butt, and lower back, muted only by the thin layer of his clothes. James finds his voice, but no words leave his lips, only pitiful cries and failed attempts to bite back screams, which seem overwhelmingly loud even as they fade when Brett drags him up the stairs. I cover my ears, but through muffled screams I can hear Seth say, "You shouldn't have let him look at that scar."

Older Brothers

In my twenties I spent too much time trying to figure out who my two older brothers were, or who they were and who they became in my life. I realize I'm supposed to say I love them no matter what, that blood is thicker than water, but I don't. What I know is they were my allies and then they were not. So now when I think of my older brothers, it's mostly of when we were children and our hurts, hunger, fear, and love bound us to one another. When I think of my father there is no love, because of his words about curiosity, because he was passive, though sometimes he took action—sometimes he hurt my brothers before they ever hurt me.

I remember when we still lived in Texas and my oldest brother, Seth, ate slowly for hours at the table after everyone else had left. He spread jam perfectly on his toast, and my father made fun of him. It irritated my father. My father mimicked the way Seth ate, the way it always took too long, the way he had a hard time knowing when to stop. Seth was so skinny though, no matter how long he made his meals last. His ribs poked out, his arms like sticks, his legs like sticks. If my father's mimicking made him cry, I didn't see it. Seth continued eating slowly, his blue eyes not widening as he chewed, though his hands trembled.

Once while we were still living in Texas, I remember being in the car in the grocery store parking lot while my father ran in alone. Seth reached up from the back seat and pulled our mother's hair as she sat in the passenger seat while she went on and on about his real father. There had been no warning, other than a quick wincing of his eyes and then his arm shooting up toward her head. He wrapped her thick coils in his tiny fingers and pulled and, at least on that day, she stopped talking shit on his father. She cried and told my father about the hair pulling when he came back to the car. Seth was silent. Both my parents told Seth he would be sent away. He would be sent to *him*, to his father. The truth was that Seth wanted to be sent to him. He wanted to go. But then he looked at our brother Ben and went still. He looked at me, his little sister who would become the actual runaway, and broke his silence. He swore he didn't want to see his real dad, that he wanted to stay with us.

I'm sure he was sad to stay. Probably he was mad for caring. A few days later he tried to feed me cat food covered in chocolate. I didn't eat it, and later, hours later, Seth got sick from our Spam dinner and wondered if he was being punished. Ben and I tried sleeping on the couch in the living room while he puked next to us because our mother thought maybe it was not the Spam. Maybe Seth had the flu. She wanted him to spread his germs to us. She wanted us all to be sick at the same time. Seth turned his head and puked in a bowl. I know now that it was his body's way of responding to his sadness, to his hurt. Seth was sad to stay.

A few weeks later, or maybe it was only days—I can't quite remember exactly when other than it was after the night of puking—Ben and I sat at the table with Seth. He was preoccupied making his doughnut last, chewing slowly as his story unfolded. He told us about his first memory. Our mother's boyfriend, the one before our dad, the one after his, beat him. Extended from the boyfriend's grasp, dangling in the air by his arm, he was beaten by a man he remembers only by the licks he inflicted upon his backside, his back, his legs. My mother's boyfriend beat Seth for taking off his shitty diaper and throwing it out of the crib when he was a baby. He beat my brother for getting rid of the shit that he'd been left in for too long. Later, Seth peed between the crib bars, having thrown off the diaper again, and the boyfriend beat him for that, too. Years later, my mother told me she didn't know about the beating, but I didn't believe her because mothers, good or bad, always have a way of knowing.

When we left Texas for Tennessee it was for God, or so that's what my mother told us. When I look back on that first year in Tennessee, I see how vulnerable Ben was and what a sweet child he had been. Back then he had dark circles, muted purple and black, beneath his large dark eyes. We looked alike and we were not large. I had the same circles.

At a church revival when Ben was six and I was five, he was very tired and fought sleep as hard as a small body can. Finally he gave in. Sweet face, not enough baby fat, and subtle purple beneath his eyes. I watched him sleep against the hard-wooden pew. He slept despite the bright lights, slept against my bony shoulder. Slept. And when our father picked Ben up from the pew, held him against his chest, one arm beneath his bottom, he awakened in a gasp from the pinches our father inflicted and the twisting motion of his rough fingers around one of Ben's thin wrists. The preacher had said no falling asleep in church. Children must stay alert to God's word—our souls could burn, too. So my father grabbed my brother up from the pew, marched us out to the car at the behest of our mother, then thrust Ben into the back seat. Within minutes, not realizing the trouble he was already in for having fallen asleep in church, Ben made it all the worse when he asked, "Mamma, can we eat now? I'm hungry. I want something good."

There was no response to Ben's request for food, and the silence in the car was palpable. Once inside our one-bedroom apartment, my parents took Ben back into the bedroom. My father beat him for falling asleep in church. I heard every sting of leather meeting Ben's six-year-old skin. Seth paced, then pleaded for the beating to end, banging his fist on the door, begging again and again for my father to stop. The beating lasted. I tucked my head beneath a couch cushion, trying to shut out Ben's screams, but I could still hear everything. Our mother encouraging our father as he struck my brother again and again. Ben gave up calling out for our father to stop and instead begged Jesus for help.

Now in my thirties, because I understand we can never go back and that things cannot be set right, I write of my older brothers as children—I speak to the children they were then. Boys. Men. I don't know how to speak to them, grown up, big brothers. I don't know them, don't care to know them. But once upon a time, many different times, there were parts of my heart that broke for them. There are parts that break still.

Haunted

When I'm eight we live in Kingsport, Tennessee, a Colonial Heights neighborhood some minutes from our last house in Blountville. Seth lives in the finished half of the basement. Ben and I, and our new baby brother Logan, sleep upstairs. Seth is nearly always bored and may feel it more acutely than the rest of us. He is twelve years old and, like all of us kids, isn't allowed to go to school or to be around kids his own age. He wishes for school every day, for friends, for things to do, to be normal. It's probably hardest for him not to go since he went through most of elementary school and knows what he's missing. I have only a limited memory of school, but like Seth, I too wish we could go.

Though Seth has a different father than the rest of us, we all call my father dad. When Seth's eighteen he will leave to go be with his father, something he'd wanted to do for all of his childhood but was too afraid to demand. It was our mother who'd made him afraid, had told him if he left he'd never be allowed to see me and Ben again. So he stayed, and his father let him because, when he was about to win custody, my mother said she'd kill Seth before letting him go. Seth's father dropped the lawsuit and went without seeing his son because he believed her, Seth's stepmother believed her, and most important the court-ordered psychologist believed her. But after eighteen years of my mother calling all the shots in his life, Seth left for his father's house back in Texas, relieved that my mother couldn't stop him. It was then, only then, that my mother revealed that the man Seth thought was his father was in fact not his biological one. "Seth," she said, "was the product of an affair."

But in the Colonial Heights house Seth lives in the basement bedroom. Upstairs there's a laundry chute hidden in the floor of a closet, and that's where all the dirty clothes go. Like feeding the baby, me and my older brothers take turns doing the laundry. The boys' clothes and towels gross me out, and washing their socks is the worst. The easiest way to get to the laundry room is to walk downstairs, through Seth's room, to the unfinished section of the basement, but I'm especially scared of his room. Seth says there are bullet holes in his walls, mudded over sloppily after a murder. He hung posters of MLB players over the holes so we wouldn't have to look at them. He says demons sometimes appear in place of the players' faces, and of course I believe him. My mother told me that demons have very evil powers, and could transform into any shape or size, but as long as my heart is right with Jesus, he would protect me.

It might be that my heart has no idea how to feel about Jesus or my lack of faith in his ability to protect me from demons that makes me pretty certain that something bad will happen in Seth's room. To avoid it I drop myself down the laundry chute—I'm the right size for it, Ben used to be, but it's too tight a squeeze for him now. Then I try to outsmart the demons by rushing through the laundry, and as soon as the washing machine gets loud enough to muffle the sound of my voice, I get beneath the chute and call out for Ben. He opens the closet and pokes his head in the chute opening, sees me and, understanding my fear, runs down the stairs, through Seth's room, and to the laundry room. He doesn't say a word as he quickly leans down beneath the chute and lets me balance my bare feet on top of his shoulders. Then he stands up, giving me just the extra height I need to pull myself up through the chute. He returns through Seth's room and back up the stairs, and I wait for him at the top step to make sure the demons don't get him either.

One time Seth and I are punished for fighting, which we do often. I am devastated by my sentence of having to spend the entire night in Seth's room. We stop fighting then because I am too scared to do anything but freeze on the bed. I lay still until the fear makes me vomit. Seth gives me a dirty t-shirt to wipe my mouth and then takes me upstairs and searches for the pink Pepto medicine that is supposed to fix nausea. I am too relieved to be out of the basement to worry about making my mother angry that I disobeyed her. I climb in my own bed in the room I share with Logan, my baby brother. He is crying, and I am grateful he's awake. I pick him up, and let him sleep next to me so I won't be alone if the demons make it out of the basement. I am sure it is for the best that the two of us stick together.

I don't know how Seth was able to get our mother to let the three of us go trick-or-treating that Halloween, but he did. I've never been before and neither has Ben, so we are both excited, and then terribly disappointed when no one on our small block answers their doors. So Seth convinces our mother to let the three of us go down to the Middle School for the Halloween celebration, which he had learned about from the flyers stuck on electrical posts on our street. When we arrive at the gymnasium it's bursting with energy, bright lights, candy wrapped in orange and black wrappers; witches and ghosts guard the doors, and the ceiling is covered with black balloons and orange streamers. There are games I want to play but need tickets for, and those cost money, which my brothers and I have very little of. The ticket lady gives each of us a few tickets for free, smiling at us as she hands them over. She whispers to another woman who is also selling tickets about the "home schooled" kids down the street. It embarrasses me that people know I don't go to school and that I haven't attended school since the first grade. I look around the gym and wonder what it would be like to play here for recess and what the hallways and classrooms are like. I stop thinking about school, classrooms, and teachers. Even at eight years old, I know I'm not going to know what it feels like to be in school again; my mother has made that clear on many occasions. She has told me that God doesn't approve of schools because they breed wickedness and disrespect and encourage children to partake in the ways of the world. "And we," she would say, "are in the world, but not of the world."

I head toward a game that gives out witch stickers; though I am a little embarrassed to be as old as I am and still wanting stickers, I can't help it. I like the shapes and the colors and, most of all, the cartoon-looking characters. Seth tells me the game with the stickers stinks and to come in the haunted house instead. I start to go in, but back out once I realize it will take all my tickets, and besides, I don't want to be afraid tonight. I sit outside the haunted house to see if the boys will come back out soon, but it takes too long and I decide to go play the sticker game after all.

As I walk across the shiny gym floor, I begin to notice all the faces around me, the other children talking with one another and laughing. I catch the eye of another little girl in the line to play my game, but I cast my eyes downward quickly when she says hello. I pretend not to hear her because I can't think of anything to say, and because I am afraid she would ask who I am, and because I don't want to explain why I don't go to school.

I'm getting close to handing the tickets over when my mother's voice is in my ear.

"I never should have let you come," she says.

She straightens up and smiles at other kids and parents standing around, then she smiles back down at me and says, "Come here, Sweetie, I need to talk to you real quick." She's wearing one of my father's navy-blue sweatshirts and a jean skirt, her frosted hair is pulled away from her face with numerous hairpins, and her blue eyes look more alert that usual. She continues to smile at everyone as we walk toward the exit and out the door. Once outside the smile fades and she lets loose my hand.

"God told me not to let you come. Now Logan is sick and I have to take him to the emergency room. This is what happens for ignoring God. I need Seth to come with me to the hospital, where is he?" she asks.

"He's in the haunted house," I reply.

"Then go get him, and Ben too, we are leaving this place."

"I can't get them. You have to have tickets and I was saving mine for the sticker game."

"You aren't playing any game. Now go back in there and get your brothers."

I go back inside the gym and over to the haunted house. I ask an older kid, who is taking the tickets, to let me in to get my brothers, not to play, because I want to save my tickets for a different game. He says everyone has to pay, so I begrudgingly hand the tickets over and enter the haunted house.

"Seth? Ben? Where are you guys?" I whisper.

"Over here feeling the brains," Ben says, "Come touch 'em."

"I can't, Mom is here and says we have to go home, and Seth has to go to the hospital with her. Logan's sick," I say.

"He is not sick. She just doesn't want us to be here," Seth suddenly whispers harshly. "I'm not leaving, you can just tell her that right now. I'm here and I'm not leaving until they close the school down for the night."

"Well, I'm out of tickets and she's just gonna get mad. We better do what she wants," I say.

"Tell her you will go to the hospital if that's how you feel. There isn't any reason for all of us to suffer when she only needs one of us to go to the hospital," Seth responds.

"Ok," I say, "but you better be ready to get in trouble."

My mother is waiting in the car with the heater set on high. It's too hot, which I think might be why my little brother is clammy and pink-faced, and maybe, like Seth said, he isn't sick at all.

"I couldn't find them. I'll go with you to the hospital, okay?" I say.

This isn't okay, and it's more than clear by the look on my mother's face.

"Fine!" she snaps.

By now Logan is in my lap and has his thumb in his mouth. He's all wrapped up in a thick baby blanket, which I begin to loosen.

"Keep him wrapped up!" my mother demands.

Instead of going to the emergency room she drives to a gas station. Through the windows I watch her slowly make her way through the short aisles. Lately I've been with Seth or Ben when the shopping is done. One of us usually waits outside with our bikes while the other one buys the groceries, and then we all dangle the plastic bags of food from our handlebars for the ride home. It's odd watching my mother pick things up, look at them for a price, and then put them back down. I go ahead and loosen the blanket around Logan, letting his sweaty skin breathe, as I continue to watch my mother through the glass, the bright florescent lights reflecting off her hair and skin. It's easy to see everything she does because the sky is so dark, and the moon is covered by clouds, leaving its glow a muted silver. Her thin lips are curved downwards, her pale skin so milky, and part of me feels my mother's vulnerability as if it were my own. It's an uncomfortable, raw feeling, which makes me suddenly tired and aware of how much holding the baby is making my arm hurt. I try putting his head on my shoulder, but he doesn't like being held that way and instantly lets out long, quiet whimpers. I put him back in a cradle position and he smiles, coos a little, and I can't help but kiss his cute face.

My mother decides against going to the emergency room, after all. In the coming years she will become set against traditional medicine. Doctors and hospitals will be like dirty words and seen only when absolutely necessary, and my younger siblings will not be immunized or seen for check-ups. But for now, my mother simply decides Logan is doing better, takes both of us back to the house, puts Logan in his crib, and tells me to go to bed as well. As she pulls the bedroom door nearly closed she says, "I'm going back to get your brothers out of that place. Halloween is Satan's holiday; I can't believe I let you all manipulate me into thinking it was something innocent. Go to sleep."

She doesn't give me time to protest or explain my fear of being left alone in the house, and I probably wouldn't know how to tell her anyway. She's gone. As soon as she is out the door Logan cries. I pick him up because I'm scared if he makes any noise the demons will know we are home. Seth says they won't come upstairs if they think the house is full of people. I have a sinking feeling that it won't take the demons long to figure out that me and Logan are home alone, and as soon as they figure that out, we are done for. They will take us both into a space where there is no light streaming through windows or trees with breezes that run through their branches, and blood will ooze from the wounds they inflict, and there will be darkness that hides hands and fingers reaching for flesh, gripping it, forcing it to be still while they feed. So I put Logan in the bed with me, which calms him. I try to hide under the covers, but he keeps giggling and squirming. I decide I can't stop him, so take hold of his little calf and let him scootch around as much as he wants. I don't move at all, except for when Logan gets too close to the edge of the bed, which I know by the way his little leg tugs against my grip. Then I sit up real fast and pull him back close to me. This happens over and over until I'm half tempted to make him a bottle to keep him still, but my fear of leaving the bed is too great, and so I keep holding onto his leg and let him move around at will. He almost falls again, and this time when I sit up, make the mistake of looking at the doorway. There is something there. I'm sure it's a demon and scream out for help, calling Ben's name.

"What are you screaming for? And why is the baby out of his crib? Just let him cry himself to sleep for once!"

I recognize my mother's voice. She walks toward the bed and takes Logan from me and places him in his crib. Immediately he begins to cry.

Dirty Water

I started working as a river guide in the Grand Canyon in my early twenties, back in 2001. Like most river guides, I drink too much. Some years are worse than others. The last summer I guided I was in my thirties and had an academic position at a university, but I also had, still have, a thing about not burning bridges with any consistent paying job. Growing up poor has its lasting effects. That last summer was rougher than most, I suppose because I didn't really want to be working the river anymore—the clients could make it miserable, co-workers could too, and if I'm being honest, so could I. Despite all the bullshit though, there was always the river, always the Canyon that helped save me by giving me something beautiful and massive to take up space in my head. The Canyon has a way of making one feel small in all the good ways, and it distracted me from the childhood I left back in Tennessee when I needed distraction most.

After that last season when I left the river to return to the "rim world," I kept up my drinking habits right up to the start of the semester. One afternoon I drank with new friends well into the night. One friend stayed sober and drove me home because I could not. The motion of the car and lack of food brought the booze up—all liquid. I ran a shower, a hot rinse. Then I sat in the tub while it filled, leaned back, and fell to sleep. I woke up shivering, added hot water and went back to sleep. At some point, after hours of draining some cold water and adding hot between sleeps, I dragged myself out of the tub and crawled into my bed. I was wide awake and I felt like shit. I stared at the ceiling and thought of the time my mother woke me up saying, "I saved my bathwater for you—get in while it's still warm."

I'm ten years old and she leaves the bathroom while I sleepily let my underwear fall to the floor then pull my nightgown over my head. I wear the same gown almost every night—it's one of my favorite things. The once soft material is now rough and has tightened around my wrists and neck over the years, so the elastic in the fabric now leaves pink rings around my skin. On the front of the gown is a picture of a girl with braids; she wears a big smile and is surrounded by a rainbow of words that say "Daddy's Little Girl."

I don't want to get into the water because it looks murky and gross. I try not to think of my mother's dead skin, hair, and dirt floating in the water. I get in and the water is barely tepid and small shivers take over my body, so I curl onto my side and try to get underneath as much of the shallow water as possible. It warms me a little but only for a minute. I lean my head against the porcelain of the tub only to discover it's cold where it remains untouched by water. Despite the cold, my body demands more sleep, pulls me into a kind of awake, yet not awake state of being. My eyelids break through their heaviness when my mother jerks my arms out of the water and tells me to get out, to be modest and wrap up in the towel. The towel, like my mother's bathwater, is used. It smells faintly of must and shampoo, clings to my body, especially to my hips and flat chest.

"You can't sleep in the tub. You could have drowned," my mother says.

"I didn't mean to," I reply.

I look in the mirror above the sink. I think my hair looks dirtier than it had been the day before. My lips are blue and my teeth chatter, and the thought of chores leaves me more tired than ever.

"Get dressed. Noah needs to be fed," my mother says.

Rest is hard to come by, especially after nights of Noah's crying, so sleeping in the tub had been easy to succumb to. The sound of babies crying hurts my body—I hate it. To quiet Noah, just as when Logan was a baby, I put him in the bed with me to soothe him. Still, I don't know what's worse, the sound of his crying, my fear of rolling on him in my sleep, or his falling off the bed and hitting the soft spot on his head. At least it's morning and both of us survived another night, I think while I buckle Noah into his car seat, tuck a cloth underneath his tiny chin, and begin to feed him. He giggles and smiles a lot. He is a very pretty baby and I think that must mean that all of us kids were cute babies since we all look so much alike. Although I can't be sure because there aren't many photos of me as a baby, but the ones of Seth and Ben reveal them to have been very cute, which I admire, though I feel a little mad that there are only the ones of me in the hospital at birth and another few when I was six months old.

I start out feeding Noah slowly. He spits a lot of the cream-colored food out and by the time he is a quarter of the way through with the jar, his face is pink from where the food dripped on his skin and from me wiping at it with a diaper cloth. I get bored feeding him and start to give him bigger bites and he spits out even more, which makes me angry with him, and he responds to my anger with a devastated look. I feel so bad that I put the food away, clean him up, tickle his tummy, and take him to the living room to play in his playpen. He throws his toys over the playpen walls, and they land on and around me where I lie reading. At first he giggles, but then squeals with irritation when he realizes he doesn't have any more toys to throw, so I toss them back in the pen. He gets excited when I move because he thinks it means I'm going to pick him up. He throws all the toys out again, and this time when I give them back, he just sits down and cries. I give in and take him out of the playpen but quickly forget about him, becoming mesmerized by my book, until Seth walks sleepily in the living room with Noah in his arms.

"Who is supposed to be watching him?" he asks.

"I don't know. I guess you are," I say, hoping to be left alone with my book.

"No, I'm not. I just woke up. You are supposed to be watching him, aren't you?"

"Nope."

"Mom, Rachel isn't paying attention to Noah and he's crawling all over the place," Seth yells in the direction of the hallway that leads to the three bedrooms.

"Rachel, I told you to take care of your brother!" she yells back from her bed.

I throw my book across the room and stomp toward Seth. "Give him to me then."

He wears a smirk on his face and hands Noah to me. I think about how much easier things had been before Logan and Noah were born. Then I look at Noah's face and see that his beautiful brown eyes intently search my face. I'm hit with pangs of guilt, tell him I'm sorry, kiss his cheeks, and try to make him laugh.

When my father comes through the front door after working his graveyard shift, me and Noah are still alone in the living room, Seth having returned to the room he shares with Ben and Logan. My father is clearly struggling to keep his eyes open, but he sees my book lying on the floor and asks what I'm reading.

"It's on the Civil War, a girl's journal," I tell him.

His worn eyes brighten, showing a hint of interest; he likes any kind of war history, which I think must stem from his father having fought in Vietnam. My father doesn't know that I took his father's Purple Heart from his dresser and keep it hidden beneath my bed. Sometimes I take the medal out and touch it gingerly, imagining that my grandfather wonders about me. (Eventually, I will meet him, the only time I'll see or talk to him, and he will dismiss me like a nuisance after instructing me to keep Logan from running around the place like a "wild Indian." I'll decide my grandfather is an ass and think very little of him for the rest of my childhood.) For now, my own father takes Noah from me, plays with him briefly, and then asks if my mother is still in bed, to which I answer in the affirmative. He gives Noah back to me and starts to walk down the hallway toward their bedroom.

"Dad?"

"Yeah?"

"Do you think you and I could go to breakfast sometime after you get off work, just you and me?"

"Sure. We can go tomorrow."

"Really? Just us?"

"Just us," he says as he turns his back to me and walks down the hallway.

In the evening when my father has gone back to work, my mother calls me to their bathroom and asks me to read a pregnancy test. She is almost certain she is pregnant again but can't be sure if the line is blue enough. I tell her I think it is.

"Good," she sighs.

I've gotten used to her asking me to do strange things. The last time she had me look at a pregnancy test it confirmed that she wasn't pregnant. She told me she was sure she had been pregnant a couple of months before when she got a very heavy period that had not really been like a period at all. I wasn't sure what to say to her, so I asked her what she did with the baby. She said she miscarried and there was lots of blood clots with the dead baby, who didn't even look like a baby and she flushed it all down the toilet. Trying to keep from picturing all the blood and chunks of dismembered parts floating in the water proves difficult, but when I think of my mother sitting on the toilet, I'm quickly able to erase the images from my mind because I hate thinking about her body; the way she represents herself as weak because she is female turns my stomach. So I think of the book I've been reading, the one with the girl, like many, who kept a journal of her time during the Civil War. Like many girls during the war, she had wounds that came from outside of the body, wounds that did not consist of bloody pieces of would-be babies, wounds that sometimes came from loneliness. Their wounds were not made up for attention. I think my mother must suspect I'm not listening, not engaging fully with her words, though she doesn't confront me; instead she brings me back to the present moment with a jolt.

"I thought I might be pregnant again this month because my period didn't come, even when I put a tampon in to help it start," she says, her eyes unwavering on my face.

When she tells me this I nod my head, look at the floor, hide my disgust. At ten years old, I'm not certain about the mechanics of tampons, but even I know they don't start periods. She has told me that they hurt, but I try not to listen to those details. One of the first times she gave me intimate and unwanted information was at the grocery store bathroom. She took a tampon out of her purse, handed me the purse, and made me face the wall while she sat on the toilet.

"Oh, it hurts," she said.

I didn't say anything. I wished I could go back out in the store with Seth and Ben. I didn't want to be in the bathroom and tried to distract myself from her voice by straining my ears to hear the boys. I was sure they were running up and down the aisles, playing, one of them pushing Logan in the stroller and the other pushing the food cart.

"Did you hear me? I said it hurts."

"Yes, I heard you. I don't know what to do is all," I said.

"God, I should have left you outside the door," she replied.

"No, that's not true, Mama, I'm sorry it hurts."

I didn't know why I said that to her. I didn't want to be in that bathroom with her and didn't like being told these strange things, but was starting to realize that I was the only one she thought she could tell, so I tried not to show how uncomfortable she made me, tried not to show how much I resented her forced closeness with me.

I pick out clothes for tomorrow's breakfast with my dad and lay them out next to my bed, a favorite navy-blue sweatshirt and hand-me-down wranglers. My mother comes into the room and asks why I'm picking out clothes.

"Dad said he would take me to breakfast in the morning. Just us, and I want to be ready when he gets home. I already set my alarm."

"Oh, don't worry about the alarm. I'll wake you up. That way Noah won't wake up too," my mother says, reaching for the off switch on my alarm clock.

"Well, okay. Are you sure you will remember to wake me up?" I ask, trying not to appear worried.

"Of course. Now get to bed."

The next morning, I awake to streams of sunlight peering through the blinds and right away know I have overslept. Noah is rubbing his eyes and starting to coo from behind the crib bars. I jump out of bed and run to the living room and look out to the street for my dad's car, an old, maroon Oldsmobile that he had gotten in a trade for some carpentry work. It isn't there so I decide he must have had to work late. I go back to my room and get dressed, carefully brush my hair back into a ponytail, and then change Noah's soaked diaper. I make a bottle of formula and lay next to him on the couch as he grips the bottle with his tiny fingers, his lips hungrily wrapped around the nipple.

My mother walks through the door first, followed by my father. She is wearing actual clothes instead of a robe, her hair is curled, and there is makeup on her face. I look at them confused and then ask, "Are we going to breakfast now, Dad?" My mother answers before he can say a word.

"I tried to wake you up. I called for you three times, but you never stirred, so I took your father to breakfast."

"But I didn't hear you. Why didn't you shake me awake like you usually do?" I ask, looking at my mother.

"I told you, I called out and you never stirred. Is that all you fed Noah, a bottle?" she asks.

"Yes," I answer, this time staring straight at my father, who avoids my eyes and instead shifts his focus from my mother to the baby in my arms.

"Well, give him a jar of food, too," my mother says.

Histories

I was an MFA student in my mid-twenties when my aunt Lexie found me online. She had been looking for me and wanted to know that I was okay; she also wanted me to know that when I was born, the first niece and granddaughter in the family, everyone had been excited. She was nineteen when I was born and bought me frilly dresses, but my mother would not let me have them. I didn't know my aunt—my mother had not allowed us to know her. Now she told me about my mother as a child, a teenager, an adult. The way she could never get along, hated her stepfather, went after her sister's boyfriends. My aunt only told me these things because I asked, because I wanted to know what my mother was like before she married my father. I had pushed my aunt to say more than the "she always had problems," she initially offered. It was this conversation, along with pieces of my mother's history, along with what I'd pieced together about my father, that helped me construct their history. It's a way of mapping out the past and where I come from. I think I've figured out my parents' history, but I can't say so with complete certainty.

My father is a small boy, maybe eleven, maybe younger, and he lands solid punches on the cheek, jaw, and nose of another boy his age. The fight is over something neither boy remembers, but they each feel rage about something that has nothing to do with the other. The other little boy's rage quiets as he's made weak from the beating my father gives him. Pain takes over and he huddles on the ground, covers his face as he knows so well how to do, while my father drives his foot into the boy's ribs. Up until this point, until that thick, awful sound of my father's sneakered foot meeting the flesh and bone of the boy, my grandfather watched the fight proudly from the window. My father doesn't know what it means to be beaten when down, or perhaps he does. But whether it was the not knowing or not caring what it was like to be curled like a fetus on the ground, covering face with bruised limbs while another body whaled upon every unprotected place, he would quickly come to learn how "real men" behave. My grandfather teaches him—how fast he ran out the front door, strong arms ready to grab his adopted child. And he did, holding my father high in the air from his forearms, his angry spit spewing in his face as he says, "Never kick a man once he's down."

The year my mother was born in the South, brutal and blustering white men murdered Emmett Till and got away with it, leaving his mother to mourn over his unrecognizable body. Some forty years later my face went hot with shame each time I heard my mother use the Bible to justify her belief that interracial marriage was wrong and that "most slave holders of the south treated slaves like family." Now, as an adult, I understand why the only Black parents in our neighborhood did not allow their children to play with me. And later, when I was a teenager and my mother beat my little brother behind a locked door that I was not strong enough to break down and no amount of my pleading made her stop, it occurred to me just what family meant to my mother.

Her whole life my mother liked soft fabrics, lace, things in pink—romantic things, she called them. When she became a mother, she still found the greatest beauty in porcelain, in landscape paintings, in furniture, like the bed she bought for me, the one she refused to give up. She had a beautiful bedroom set once, then the store came and took it back because the payments had stopped some time before. She tried not to cry when my father brought home an ugly Goodwill bedroom set. At least it was furniture, he had said. I felt bad for her then, I wanted her to have the things that made her happy, I wanted her to take the furniture she had put in my room, but she wouldn't. Later she reminded me of all her sacrifices, the kind her mother wouldn't have made for her. She was quick to remind me how lucky I was to have the parents I had because it could have been worse; I could have had parents like hers. I wonder if my grandmother had tried to force-feed her medications not prescribed to her or asked what she'd done to make boys touch her body, as my mother asked me when I'd told her what I'd suffered at the hands of my older brothers.

When I was fifteen my father took me on a drive and told me if I just hung on at home a little longer, took care of the "house" just a little longer, he'd help me finally get an education. Then he dropped me off at the house and I heated Tater Tots for my little brothers' dinner.

Over the years I was growing up, my father gripped me by the forearms so tightly I could feel the blood pulsating in my veins, trying hard to push past his fingertips. But he held fast, and held my eyes with his, trying to force me to look away, to look down. Sometimes, a lot of times, especially when I was a young child, I did cast my eyes down. Then he would release his grip, only then, for he felt submission had been won. But really, I hated him for it. I didn't know where he learned this thing of staring down an animal or a child until they submitted, but now I suspect it was from his own father. And maybe it's why he was so in love with god-awful movies where horses nodded yes to real men and so did the soft-skinned women. His children only looked away from him because it meant being let go and, hopefully, let alone.

Birth control pills were not approved by the Food and Drug Administration until '61 and safe abortions were nearly impossible to come by in the state of Texas until '73. At the end of the fifties my grandmother was raped and impregnated by her husband, days after giving birth to their third child. As a young girl I overheard my mother, who would spend much of her day on the telephone, wondering about the boys her mother had given up for adoption. She spoke of them in a hushed tone. Maybe my mother remembers seeing her father, the man who spent much of his life in prison, as a force of violence, but to her that was not his greatest crime. My aunt Elena was still fresh to the world, not quite four days old when my grandmother brought her home from the hospital. My grandfather had been waiting. He goes after her as soon as my grandmother puts Kitty in the bassinette. My grandmother is nineteen years old when she is thrown to the floor and raped. I wonder if my mother saw it. Was she so close to violence the force of it vibrated the floor beneath her feet? Did she hide in the corner? Under the bed? Did she scream or did she cry silently? Did she understand what was happening? Maybe she wasn't even there while her mother waited for her father to get so drunk he passed out, and then she got up from the floor with blood running down her legs and fled to Dallas.

As a child of a single mother with disabilities, my father grew up eating meals made possible by taxpayers. All throughout my childhood my father refused to take government welfare. "Taking handouts from the government is a sin," he'd say. When I was twelve my family of eight lived in a two-bedroom trailer in Sullivan County, Tennessee, and nearly every night for dinner the children ate popcorn. To this day I cannot stand the smell of the stuff. My father was poor when he was a kid and stayed poor or damn near it his whole life. But when his father walked out and he was still a child, having no money did something to his pride. His half-deaf, partially blind mother did her best, I'm sure. She loved him, I know. Maybe not enough. Maybe not the way he wanted. She always referred to him as her adopted son when making introductions. But if his mother's love was not enough, he never said as much to me. Not that that means anything. He was good at silence.

In the sixties it became illegal to openly pay women less than men doing the same job. In the eighties, when my parents met and quickly married, my mother informed my father she would not work, that it was his job to support her and her job to make a home. When I was six my then family-of-five lived in a one-bedroom apartment, and my mother cried because she was embarrassed to wear her only dress to church yet again. My mother said her stepfather would never buy her presents, but every payday he took her stepsister, his biological daughter, shopping. Maybe this is where my mother's desire for things comes from, things for herself, and certain kinds of things for her children. She said her stepsister was given gifts and she and her sisters given backhand slaps to the face. Her stepsister says the claims are false, are cruel. Maybe my mother wanted to demonize the man that replaced her father or maybe he really didn't treat her as his own, the way he treated her stepsister. Who can say? But what's for certain is that she held on to her little-girl-self telling her biological father goodbye. She struggled most of her young life, trying to make sense of the father she wished for and the one she had.

Way back in the 1790s Mary Wollstonecraft called for the equal education of women. She pushed back hard on men's depiction of women as weak yet cunning creatures that must be bridled. She argued for the vindication of women's rights. Centuries later, I went through my teenage years hearing my mother bashing educated women she perceived as feminists, nonsubmissive bra burners.

My father's mother didn't have money to wash the clothes, so she washed them in the bathtub. Being poor didn't get any easier with age, either. Once, when I was twelve, my father sat my older brothers and me down and told us how he had to beg a loan from a rich man. He begged. He said he was pathetic. I didn't understand why he told us about the loan, but if he meant for us to feel shame with him, I did. I remember that rich man; he and his family lived in a blue house and owned horses. On the way over to pick up the loan, my mother said nasty things about his wife. When my parents started fighting, yelling about money and everything else, I noticed my mother's hand reach for the door handle. My father had started driving faster when the yelling began, so I reached up from the back seat and held my hand over the lock of my mother's door, pressing it as hard as I could. He pulled over, grabbed her arm, and stared. After that the drive was silent, my father pulled up next to the blue house and both parents told me I had to stay in the car while they went inside. But when I saw the rich man guide them out the door and toward the barn, I slipped out of the hot car and walked to the house. The woman my mother had said nasty things about opened the door before I had a chance to knock. She leaned down and held me tight.

Of all the crimes reported in Texas during the sixties, three were tied to my grandfather, but the rape of my grandmother was not one of them. It wasn't until the seventies that the first state, Nebraska, declared it illegal for husbands to rape their wives, and, slowly, over nearly two decades, other states followed suit. Missouri and North Carolina were the last to do so.

My mother remembers when her mother returned from Dallas to collect her girls from my great-grandmother. Then she drove my mother and her sisters to their father for a final goodbye. Maybe he winked at my grandmother as he signed the divorce papers and said something like, "You sure you want to walk away from me?" And she might have said, "Just sign the papers, Junior." My grandmother was young, somewhere around twenty-three years old, with auburn hair, blue eyes, and lips covered in a dark red hue. Her body was slender but built strong. A cigarette loosely dangled between her tobacco-stained fingers, and a thin line of smoke curled up from her hand. My mother's hair was in tight ringlets that bounced and shone blond under a Texas sun as she watched her daddy lean over the hood of the car signing papers. She ran to him when her mother said it was time to go, held on hard to his leg and insisted she would not leave him. But he picked her up, stroked her face, told her what a pretty thing she was as he sat her in the back seat, and then shut the car door behind him.

When I was about eight years old, my father enrolled in college courses, but dropped out within a year. He mocked the students who were more than ten years younger for their stupidity and for their fancy cars that were nicer than his and for the jobs they would take that should be his. Later, I recall that my father's car died on the way up a hill to church. It blocked traffic and when people in nicer, running cars went around us, he looked at them and when they looked back said, "Yeah, go ahead and look at me like I'm trash," but they didn't hear him. And when some of those same people later saw us pull into the church parking lot, he smiled at them. He joked about the car being on its last wheel and that he'd been meaning to get a new one, just hadn't found the time to get down to the dealer. I'd felt bad because I knew it killed him a little to say that, to put on that face, to joke about buying a car he couldn't afford.

In the early 1970s the prison population hadn't yet reached a quarter of a million. Around that same time my mother visited my grandfather in a Texas prison where he would serve a multi-decade sentence. When I was fifteen, my five-year-old brother, when provoked, displayed a violent temper, which made my mother gasp with both horror and pride. She claimed he was like her father and one day he too might see the inside of a prison cell.

Ten years passed and my mother didn't see her father, not since the day he lifted her into my grandmother's car and walked away. She visited him in prison where he was serving his sentence for manslaughter. He did not love her the way she wanted him to, he did not love her at all, or at least he didn't show it, and that, not the violence and killings, is what finally made her close the door on him.

My father has a brother, but I don't know him. He's adopted too. He didn't live at home as long as my father did, I suppose. Though in the end I'm guessing it was my uncle, not my father, that did most of the tending of their mother in her last days. Maybe I'm wrong. Maybe I like thinking the worst of my father, and maybe I do that because it makes the most sense. I once overheard him tell my older brother he understood why he "did stuff" to me because I was a girl, and boys couldn't help being interested in girls. I wonder if that's the kind of line he used to defend himself when he was caught harassing the woman who, after some months, ended their affair. Men can't help what they do when they are "interested." As of 2002 something like 2 percent of sibling abuse is reported. Who is there to tell? And which child will parents determine is most worth protecting?

Near the time my mother was to enter high school, images of American soldiers massacring a village of Vietnamese civilians surfaced—children and babies killed at the hands of grown and nearly grown men, women and girls raped by the same, and the old had their lives snuffed out in a fury of meaningless violence. When I was a child and saw a group of young people gathered near our small courthouse protesting the Gulf War, my mother told me they displayed rebellion, and rebellion was a sin she had never been guilty of. When thousands protested the Vietnam War, my mother had not joined them.

My mother caught me looking at a photo of her when she was in high school. She had gorgeous thick hair and the most beautiful hands with long fingernails. I was rough, a girl with bitten nails and rashes on my hips from carrying the children she kept having. As I looked at the photo, she pointed out that even after having a child, which she did soon after high school, she was thinner than me. But I wasn't wondering about her looks and why I wasn't delicate; I just wanted to know what it was like to go to school. She wouldn't let me go because she said everything I needed to know was in the home. I learned how to do laundry, how to clean house until my skin was raw, how to tend children, how to hide the books she tried to take away, and how to count only on myself to fend off unwanted hands when they were in the mood to torment my body. I learned that my mother needed to make me into something so useless I'd never be able to leave her.

When I was twelve years old, my father took voluntary layoff. He said something about there being less work after the Gulf War, a war he'd been proud to support. Eventually, when I became a teenager, my father found a job in another factory and within a year or so he'd moved us to the outskirts of rural Rogersville, Tennessee, where I would not last even two years before becoming a teen runaway.

I once saw my father through the window of our neighbors' house. I was sitting at the piano, fingers pressing softly, as if that would quiet my mistakes. My father had started out walking angrily, but by the time he reached the neighbor's driveway he had somehow, strangely, humbled himself. The neighbor walked out to meet him, to say I was getting better at playing the piano and did he want to come in and listen. My father looked at his feet, spoke softly when he declined, and asked the neighbor to tell me to come home when I'd finished. I think my father must have come over there to grab me, probably he was mad about the children being rowdy, probably they weren't listening to him, and probably my mother was pissed that I was across the street. But when confronted with someone who seemed to treat me like a person in my own right, though of course my neighbor too had his agenda, my father changed. I just sat at the piano bench and watched him walk away and thought, *for a poor man with hungry children he sure has a big belly.*

Babies

I did not fully comprehend what my mother meant when she said she was getting a tubal ligation reversal. I was seven years old at the time, and within a year of the surgery she was pregnant with her first child since my birth. At first, I was excited. I didn't understand the work that these new children would bring with them, the way they would shape my life, how tired I'd become tending to them, or how much more I'd love them than I thought it possible to love. How I'd know what every cry meant, and the memories of each one of them would trigger a visceral reaction in me for all the years after I left them—a mix of guilt and loss and pain, of knowing they finished growing up and I was not there.

When the first baby was still in my mother's womb, I longed for it to be a sister, wanting more than anything not to be the only girl anymore. So when Logan was only hours into the world I looked at him with such disappointment. He wore a blue beanie on his tiny baby head. I asked the nurse if she was out of pink ones. "It's a boy," she said. I hated my new brother immediately. My body got hot with the disappointment of still being the only girl, a new anger boiled deep inside me. I walked away from the nurse and sat in front of the cartoons playing in the lobby. I didn't watch, not really, instead concentrating on not crying. That was most important—not to let down my anger with tears. I hated my new brother for being a boy and, later that day, only bothered to look at him when his diaper was being changed just to be sure he was in fact a boy. *Maybe the nurse made a mistake*, I thought. There was no mistake. He was boy and I hated him. But then the nurse insisted upon handing him to me. I held my brother for the first time and instantly my eight-year-old arms turned protective while resting his little head inside them and I loved him—beautiful, perfect Logan.

Over the years, Logan grew to love God. He'd been trained for that. The converts, our parents, trained him for that. He was given a saint—it was the saint of his own name and he loved him. So when his head broke open beneath the concrete of his fall, he prayed to his saint. I told him to do it. It made him feel better. I told him to do it even though I didn't believe. That's all I could do while pressing my hands against the split in his head, his eyes wide, trying so hard to be brave. He whispered to a dead man, his saint, now nothing more than bones in the ground. My eyes searched for the phone to call for help. Logan got nervous because he sensed my nervousness, but I told him it was alright, to keep talking to his saint. And he did, calling out louder than he meant to. And I held tighter to his six-year-old head, reaching for a towel to stop the blood pooling between my fingers.

Not long after Logan got hurt he asked me to teach him to read. We had no teachers because our mother did not allow us to have them, did not allow us to go to school. Logan struggled over the letters. I struggled to teach. I was not a teacher. He struggled. I struggled. I failed. Stopped teaching. He stopped asking me to teach. I let him down. When he grew up he said he had forgotten how I let him down, but I had not forgotten and I reminded him. And he said, in his perfect voice, "It's alright."

I think of my baby boy brother in the blue hat who, for a moment, was not loved by me because he was not a sister, and how he grew to be very tall, and now we are not close. It's my fault.

When Noah arrived, not even two years after Logan, I'd decided there was something in being the only girl and I didn't mind that he, too, was a boy. I was the first sibling to hold him, my father had insisted, hoping to squash the dislike he was sure I was forming for this new baby. I was glad to hold Noah, proud to be the first to hold him. In time, I'd discover that like me, Noah had a temper, so when he was around four years old, I taught him how to run like a looney toon to help him cope with the rage already building up inside his baby body. Our mother said he was not right, said he might grow to kill. There had been a pleasure in her voice when she said those words, pleasure in the horror, but I knew she was not right. So I taught him how to wind up, arms back, leg pulled up high, and zoom out of the room. And he did, too, but always just before he fled his dark eyes would look back to me, making sure I was watching, and zoom—he was gone. The first time I taught him to run like that I saw the heat flash across his face and grabbed him just before he flew into a rage, his little fists ready to hit the first thing that got in his way. I grabbed him up—he was so light. "Quick, this is how you should run. Like this," putting him down, I wound up, like a looney toon—and flew out of the room. And later, when I ran that last time, I knew he was watching from the corner and so I did not look. I did not look back as he always did.

Luke, who had joined us in the world not two years after Noah, had also watched the day I ran, but he did not have a temper like Noah's back then. He was a quiet and gentle child. He wet his pants often. He wet the sheets, too. He was wet a lot. Sometimes he would wake me up, "Rachie, I don't know what happened. My sheets are wet." So I'd get him dry clothes and try to hide the wet sheets until I could wash them the next day. Our mother called him "little pee boy," and to this day I hate her for it.

Sometimes he would try to hide his wet pants by sitting in the corner until they dried against his skin. If I was on it that day, I'd notice first. We would hide the pants together and he would whisper, "I don't know what happened."

When Luke was very little, about two years old, he got pink eye. I woke him up in the middle of the night with a warm damp washcloth in hand, wiping away the green gunk from his eyes. He cried, "No, Rachie, please no." I wiped away the gunk. He cried. And in the morning, I would wake up to his face, one eye caked shut, the other staring at me, his thumb in his mouth, free hand playing at the lobe of my ear—"It's time to wake up," he'd say. I'd sit up and go to warm the cloth beneath water, and he would cry out, "No, Rachie, please no."

When Luke was a baby, I had rashes on my hips from carrying him everywhere. It was like this*:* he didn't like anyone else to hold him. He cried when our mother tried to take him from me.

When he grew and saw me run out the door the day I left home for good, he didn't cry, just stared at me. And still, I ran.

I don't know that Michael saw me leave, but I suspect he did. I do know that he was perhaps the sweetest tempered child that has ever been born into this world, though he was no pushover. His hair was long and fine—a yellow blond, and when I cut it, he cried out. "I hate it. I hate it!" He squealed and squirmed. In truth, his hair did look as though a butcher went at it with a dull knife. I felt ashamed of the job I'd done. But he ran to the mirror in his overalls and red shirt, shook his head, the fine threads a small yellow storm, and giggled, "I don't hate it now!"

When Michael laughed it was perfect, the sound of it like happy water. I remember his laugh most, and his sweet voice, but I don't remember his favorite toys or games, and that's not right. I do remember that I called him Bobbygushnick and put scarves around his face and told him if he were an old lady he would have to wear one every day to keep his hair just so, and this made him laugh and I kissed his face.

When my little sister Samantha finally arrived, six years after Logan was born, and about a year and a half after Michael came into the world, it was so late I almost didn't care that she was a girl. I didn't know what to do with a sister, fourteen years younger than me. Our father made a makeshift room for her right next to mine. The walls were a horrid peach color and there were holes in the floor. There were holes in the floor where a clawfoot tub had once stood, another where there had been a toilet. Our father covered the holes by nailing boards over them, imprecise cuts of yellow plywood.

I knew that it wasn't right to put babies in bed with their bottles, but I was too tired to hold another kid, and there were times I put her in bed with one anyway. I crept away from the peach walls and the yellow boards. I was afraid she would cry. And she should have cried when I left her there alone, but she only softly whimpered when she awoke. Her whimpers were determined though—her arms taut and reaching up, her legs taut, toes pointing straight to nothing—a silent anger. She clung to my neck each time I picked her up until, eventually, I could never put her back in that peach room with the yellow boards. So I held her with tired arms. Rashes on my hips. And it was right.

When I snuck back to see my baby siblings something like a year after running away, there was dirt stuck to my sister's face and hands, and her brown curls were a matted mess. So I washed her and she smiled. I washed her and brushed out the mess and she smiled, even as long threads of her knotted hair were pulled loose, limply falling from the comb to the floor. And when finally I cried, she did not smile but reached up and touched my face. It was like this: when the runaway cried, Samantha reached up, while Michael and the rest of the boys pushed close, little hands patting my arms and legs.

After Birth

While my mother is pregnant with Logan, she grows concerned that I'm not soft enough, not enough of a "lady," so she enrolls me in ballet classes. By the time Luke breaks free of the womb, just a day after my eleventh birthday, I'm as rough as ever, though still I dance—it makes me strong. The ballet studio I attend is inside an old warehouse in Kingsport, Tennessee. Its walls are painted powder blue or covered with mirrors to reveal every angle of dancing bodies, but the windows have not been updated beyond coats of blue paint on the rebar in front of them. On the other side of the barricaded windows a train runs by. I feel the vibrations in the floor as train car after train car passes the studio. The sound of old iron screeching against new steel cancels out the classical music playing on a record as I loosen my grip on the barre—attempt a balance and fall.

I'm in a ballet class when my mother goes into labor with Luke, as I discover when it's not my father who waits for me but Angie, the realtor. She is trying to sell our house before the bank repossesses it. Unlike my father, she comes inside the studio to wait for me, sits patiently in the lobby. She looks worried, which tells me all I need to know. I don't even bother asking how she got roped into picking me up because I know there is no one else, that she is the only adult who interacts with my parents on a regular basis. She won't last. They never do.

"Your mother's gone into labor," she says.

"Is it going to be here soon?" I ask.

"Yes, very soon, but there are complications and the midwife was late."

I know I'm supposed to be concerned for my mother, but I'm not.

The arrival of the new baby means more work, and, no doubt, will mean missing ballet rehearsals. This is especially upsetting because I'm an "Hour" who jumps out of the clock in time with Prokofiev's warning symbols to tell Cinderella her time is running out and she must flee the ball. I take my part very seriously, embracing this ballet with fascination, curious about the strike of midnight when the ball gown turns to a simple worn-out frock but the slipper remains beautiful, unblemished, a remnant of the magic that can withstand time. I don't understand the slippers and why they don't turn back to plain ugly shoes just as the gown turns to rags. It's a stupid story, a stupid ballet, but for some reason I love it—the music, the dancing, which I keep to myself. I'm learning that to show love for something makes it susceptible to being taken away.

"Thanks for the ride," I say as I get out of the car. "You don't have to come in."

"No, no, I better come see how things are going," says Angie.

Angie and I walk through the kitchen door, ears greeted with the screech of my mother's labor pains escaping from behind her bedroom walls. Seth is pacing, as he always does when nervous. I look for Ben, who doesn't seem to be around, but I see Logan, looking unkempt and playing on the living room floor. Angie sits down at the kitchen table for a few minutes, rubs her forehead nervously, and the next time my mother screams, she jumps up and flees the house. I hate and envy Angie. Hate because she's seen the way my family lives, envy because she can walk away.

The house feels gross and I feel gross being in it. The kitchen floor is speckled with dried-up liquid—dark sticky spots, and the trashcan overflows with used diapers and uneaten oatmeal from breakfast. The pale blue carpet smells like stale flowers from the recent shampoo my mother had done, hoping to induce her labor but giving up after a few minutes and making Seth finish the cleaning.

A short time ago, I'd been dancing in a fairy tale, and now I'm listening to the screams of my mother as she gives birth to another kid. The whole thing is disgusting. I brave the hallway that echoes with my mother's noise so I can get to my bedroom. I need to see Noah. He is in his crib, wide awake, tears wetting his little face, and I feel bad that I hadn't heard him crying right away. I pick him up, hold him until he calms down, and then the two of us sit together on the floor and play with his toys. Our mother gives out another horrifying scream. This time Noah doesn't mind because he isn't alone, but I mind. I grab him up quickly. He nestles down in my lap, and I rock him back and forth.

"I'm so sorry you had to be born into this family."

I tell him this over and over so many times that it starts to sound like a chant. He reaches above his head to my face, feels for my cheek, and pats it a few times. He giggles, and I hold him tighter. Ben brings a bottle for Noah and sits on the floor with us. From time to time I catch the sound of Noah gulping his formula between our mother's screams. Eventually, the noise from our parents' room quiets until my father calls for all of us to come see the new baby.

My mother is on the floor leaning against the foot of the bed, her hair is tied on top of her head, and there are speckles of blood on her nightgown and the blanket she's sitting on. Her face is red and sweat clings to her skin. The room feels disgusting, humid, and smells of bad meat and urine. She tells me to come look at the baby, our new brother, who she is holding and is seemingly mesmerized by. I have heard her say infancy is her favorite stage children go through.

"Why is its nose so flat?" Ben asks.

"It is a he, not an it," our father says.

I step closer to see what Ben is talking about. The baby's whole face is flat and his blueish skin still has traces of blood on it and so does his hair, which is dark and damp.

"Gross!" Ben yells.

My eyes dart to Ben and then to the thing he's staring at on the ground. A sack covered in blood sits in a Rubbermaid pan, and the clear bottom of the pan is covered in a shallow pool of blood.

"It's just afterbirth," our father says with annoyance.

The midwife, a figure I barely recognize (or acknowledge for that matter) moves the pan out of sight. Me and Ben look at each other, and then at the door. He leaves first and I want to follow, but I can't bring myself to leave Noah. My father is showing Noah the new baby, but he is anything but interested, and he squirms and softly whimpers, struggling against my father's firm grasp. I can see the frustration building on my father's face and decide I could probably get Noah back now.

"Here, I'll take him so you can help Mom," I say.

He gives Noah to me and I head for the door slowly, so as not to seem too eager to leave, which I know will upset my mother. But as soon as we're out of eyesight I hurry to the living room. Ben and Logan are watching Tom and Jerry cartoons. I know Ben didn't ask for permission to watch television. I know we will all be punished for watching the cartoons, but this time I don't care, and so curl up on the couch with Noah, desperate to forget the blood.

Education

All the moving and all the babies have a way of blurring time. When I think back to the beginning of Tennessee, I add it to my mental map of my family history and the years I spent with them in Appalachia. I piece together the events, I figure out how old I was when those events unfolded, I reorder them as best I can chronologically on the page—it goes against the way I experience these things now, this order. Memory doesn't work chronologically. I collect the years I lived at home next to those after I left—wondering how much the distance between the two has changed me.

When I am five, before my mother decides school is evil, and I am still in kindergarten, my mother sleeps more than she doesn't. But some afternoons she is up, heating food on the stove, and reminds me that I am her "little baby girl." It is during one of these afternoons that I tell my mother it is my turn to bring the snack for class, that everyone has to take a turn. She asks me what the other kids have brought.

"Bananas, peanut butter crackers, milk, stuff like that," I inform her.

I tell her I didn't like the milk and that I wish there were more juice boxes because milk makes me gag. She is thoughtful, then says, "We'll go to the store and pick out something special!" When it is time, she orders gingerbread man cookies from the bakery and cherry juice boxes. I think it is the most wonderful snack in the world. My teacher says it was supposed to be a nutritious snack, which hurts my pride, but my joy is not completely lost when another child in the class says my snack was the best so far. I only tell my mother what that child said when she asks what was said about the snack. She smiles, seems pleased, and tells me that my brothers and I can have a sleepover. I still have pictures of that sleepover, everyone in pajamas in the living room of the small apartment in Tennessee, the third home we've had since leaving Texas. My mother's hair is frosted, her face a smile amid a pile of children, and she actually appears happy. I look at that picture and see my tiny body curled up next to hers and remember how much I used to love my mother.

I recall being a child walking home from kindergarten. I walk up the hill to my family's apartment and it tires out my legs and my stomach growls for something to eat. Sometimes when I get home the door is locked; my mother is sleeping in the back bedroom, so I sit outside waiting, sometimes for hours, to be let in. I don't bang on the door as Seth and Ben do when they get home; I want to let my mother sleep. When the door isn't locked, I slip quietly into the bedroom, wait for my eyes to adjust to the darkness, then ease up to the bed and place my hand near my mother's nose to check for a breath. Just as carefully as

I enter the room, I leave it. In the kitchen I retrieve my favorite spoon—it has a long, narrow handle. I have heard my mother call it an iced tea stir spoon. I take it to the refrigerator and sit down on the floor crossed-legged. I eat four spoonsful of Cool Whip and then wash the spoon and put it back in the drawer. Soon I feel ill and throw up the sweetness.

When I'm eight I look six and we live in the country in Blountville, Tennessee. Out in front of the rented ranch house, I am wearing a pink sweatsuit and watch my shadow playing on the ground. I look taller, my ponytail blowing rapidly in the wind. Seth and Ben teach me how to throw a football, show me how the spin goes, spend hours with me until I get it right. I am proud when I see the ball spiral fast through the air. Pleased with myself, I go inside to fix something to eat—peanut butter toast. The bread gets jammed inside the toaster so I climb the counter top, take a butter knife to dig out the bread and am quickly sent backwards, landing on the cold linoleum. Seth walks in. "You can't stick stuff in the toaster, it shocks you," he says as he picks me up and sets me at the table. He boils water and makes a bowl of ramen noodles, sets it in front of me, and walks out of the room.

This is the same year I start ballet classes. At first, for several years, I hate it. I don't understand how to be around the other children, but my mother insists I keep at it because I don't act enough like a girl. I notice the girls doing their homework in the dressing room, so I start bringing a book with me to read while they study. Sometimes my father lets me go to the library before ballet class. He drops me there on his way to work and lets me walk to the studio. For years this is how I will learn—the books that my mother won't let me read at home will become well known to my fingers as I pull them from their shelf and read them in the safety of the stacks. As an adult, I'll pause to wonder about how I learned to find books in the library and realize it was my mother who taught me. I figure she regretted teaching me, years later, when I start bringing home books about college.

At ballet I notice the other girls have different kinds of books, different subjects they study. I try to teach myself about science. I find my father's old biology book, the one from his only semester of college. He'd been a student when I was eight years old. Now I'm thirteen and trying to understand the text in the book. The glossy pages are confusing and again I feel that familiar kind of film settle over my brain. I don't understand. But when my mother finds me reading the biology book she says, "Ha, college level and you don't even have to go to school." I don't bother telling her I don't understand the text. I know it won't make any difference and she'll only tell me it's because I don't have an aptitude for science. She uses that word so often about me and my limitations that the sound of it turns my stomach before she can finish saying it. To this day I cannot stand the word "aptitude."

I am about nine when I ask my father a question about numbers. It sets him off because it's a question no nine year old should need to ask. He stomps down to his bedroom, throws open the door and demands of my mother why I don't know math. I am filled with embarrassment, which worsens when I hear my mother say, “She doesn’t have an aptitude for math!” I am confused when I hear this because my first grade teacher had said math was my best subject. And I remember liking math the best. When my mother comes storming out of her bedroom I freeze as she brushes past me, grabs some math textbooks she had ordered some time ago but never opened, and then marches me into her room. All day she crams math into my head, by five o’clock I’ve gone through the second-, third-, and halfway through the fourth-grade math books. “Look. Now she’s more than caught up,” my mother says to my father. He’s quiet as he looks over some of my problems, tells me I need to work on my handwriting. That night as I lie in bed and Logan sleeps across from me in his crib with his little feet curled up under his tiny hips, I try to recall what it is I learned that day, but cannot. It’s as if there is a haze covering my brain. I make a promise to myself that I won’t always be behind.

When I’m ten I crack my collarbone for the first time—roughhousing with Seth and Ben in yet another house, still in the Colonial Heights area but on Lindenwood Drive. This house my parents own but will end up selling at a loss. Right now, though, my mother yells for quiet, is on the phone with some religious person, then another. Hours later she looks at my collarbone, comments on its redness, but says it’s fine. I reinjure it three weeks later—again, roughhousing. My father looks at it and makes my mother call the doctor. The doctor looks at my injury, lays me down on the table and, standing between me and my parents, speaking to them the whole time, he inspects my belly and chest, is calm when he, without letting them know, checks my privates. I didn't understand at the time, but now I know he was looking for abuse. The doctor tells my parents they waited too long to treat my break. There was little to be done but put me in a sling. Later, when I am thirteen and hurt my arm I remember the fractures in my collarbone, so don't ask for help because I know it would come at the cost of my mother's anger. Anger over the medical bill, but most especially anger about any special attention I might receive because of the injury. I hold my arm and know part of it is broken, so I do my best to protect it, but one time I wake up and discover myself sprawled out on the floor, having blacked out after accidently hitting my arm against my bedroom door in yet another house—this one on a dead-end street on the outskirts of Kingsport.

My mother is cleaning out kitchen cabinets, has me stand on a chair as she hands things up to me to place on the shelves. There are a few vases, cereal containers, two plastic lunch boxes that me and Ben have not used in nearly six years, not since we'd been pulled from school. I look at the pink one, recognizing my first name printed evenly on the front, but I'm not sure about the name following mine, so I sound it out. M-i-c-h-e-l-l-e comes out Mitchell. My mother snaps at me, "That's your middle name! How do you not know how to spell your own middle name?!" Immediately I redden in shame. I've never had to write my middle name before, and as I sit there thinking about it, it's all a blur. I read books all the time, I've probably read that name before. And I wonder if I've always read Michelle as Mitchell. I say I'm sorry, tell her I just read it wrong. I set the lunchbox aside. "I think I'll keep this in my room," I say. Later that night, while my newest little brother, Noah, sleeps in his crib across from my bed, I take the lunchbox under the covers, and with a small light, look at my middle name, bring pencil to paper, and write the middle name over and over until I have it memorized.

I'm eleven when Ben goes hunger fishing in Kendrick Creek in our Colonial Heights neighborhood. When he hooks a kernel of corn, fresh out of a can, sitting atop granite, I try to look away so he can slip a few golden pieces between his lips. I know he bites down only once before swallowing sweetness. It hurts like sickness, like cherries candied slick, to see my big brother eating bait instead of using it for a bigger catch that could get him closer to full. Why was it so hard to not be hungry? Or why, when I slip and slice my foot, broken glass under water, and a neighborhood child runs for his mother as I go on ahead toward home, leaving a bloody trail behind me, am I surprised to see my father show up? Why has he responded to that mother's call? Why does he lift me like an infant and carry me home? Is it real, his worry? And where has my brother gone? He's grown tall, past tin cans and the barely fleshed fish, red-eye and blue-gill who move swift in the shallows, lethargic in the deep.

A few years later, when my family lives in a trailer after our summer of homelessness, I don't quite recall Ben being there, aside from when he'd been hurt in a baseball game—I remember that day, him on that day, the most. It's yet another boy's mother who picks him up and drives him to the hospital. Then she finds my father and says, "Your little boy thought he was going to die, thought he would go to hell." She says, "No child should be thinking such things." And Ben sits pink faced, tear streaks like strawberry and vanilla, hand over wound. I sit up while he sleeps that night, to wake him if his breath gets weak or else he will not shut his eyes, so fear-struck of fire and Satan and all those tales of being sent down in the hot folds of earth to live with fire and weeping and the scent of impure child skin burning. It is an old story, one our mother had given up telling when the two of us were six and seven, but Ben had held that memory, fear spreading through his child heart, hurting for love.

I'm twelve when, for three months, my family is homeless, I remember being packed into our rusty Ford van and my father driving us across country. I hold my bird's cage in my lap and wonder if, like me, she gets carsick. We arrive in Missouri, just outside of Jefferson City, where my mother has made arrangements with a Christian family to stay in their unfinished mother-in-law space for a few days—one large room, an adjoining bathroom, cinder block walls, and a concrete floor. I place my bird in the bathroom, out of the way, because her chirping upsets my mother. I go outside to play with my little brothers. And when I return I find steam pouring from the bathroom door, my father running a towel across his wet hair. I run to the bathroom but am too late. The heat and steam have killed my bird, and her small yellow body looks bright in my pale twelve-year-old hands. When I pile back into the van and drive south toward Texas, I watch Missouri disappear and hate it.

The fall before I turn thirteen we are no longer homeless. My family of eight lives in a two-bedroom trailer in Church Hill, Tennessee. I go to a department store with my mother. She insists on trying on the kind of dresses she can't afford, the kind that sales people know she won't buy. She puts on a black strapless, a style I have been told is not modest to wear. She asks me what I think and I don't know what to say because it doesn't look right on her. So I tell her it looks okay, but the other dress she picked out was prettier. A hurt look comes over her face and I know I haven't said the right thing but hope she will let it go. I look in the mirror, look at the dress I'd put on and notice how it clings to my body and that I like the clinging. And then I notice how the dress reveals my collarbone that still juts out in the place it had been broken last. Like the previous time I had broken it, the injury has gone untreated. There is a painful throbbing in the center of the bone, but I learn to get used to it. I tell myself that soon enough the throbbing will dull, once the bone pulls itself all the way back together. I look up to discover my mother staring at my body in the mirror. Suddenly I feel ashamed and step away from the mirror. She doesn't look away from me as I awkwardly try to pull my jeans on underneath the dress. She watches me struggle with a smile and says, "You won't always look that good."

The winter when I'm thirteen my throat begins to hurt and swell. My mother tells me to gargle salt water and to take her echinacea and goldenseal tincture. At first I give myself the tincture only a little, but within days the pain is so bad that I take the concoction more frequently, hopeful it will kill the sickness living in my throat. I stay up for two nights straight, spitting in the sink to avoid the piercing pain that comes when I don't. I pace the hallway between spits and, forcing myself to drink more echinacea and goldenseal, each sip leaves me fighting back a painful scream. In the mirror I notice the circles under my eyes look worse than usual, open my mouth and see how one side of my throat nearly touches the other. I give up the pacing and sit down in a living room chair. The sun has risen and the babies are running about half-dressed. I don't move to tend them, instead pull a blanket under my chin and whimper. My mother hears me, yells from her room, "Rachel, are you crying!" "No," I attempt to lie. "Great. Rachel's crying," my mother says to my father. My father, who had just come home from a graveyard shift, enters the living room and asks if he should take me to the doctor. Through tears I tell him I'm okay, but give him a look that I hope shows I'm not okay at all. I hear my mother yelling about being manipulative and just wanting his attention. I ignore her and quickly put my shoes on, afraid my father will change his mind. He doesn't, and at the doctor's office I'm injected with steroids. The doctor tells my father he'd like to send me to the hospital but knows he and my mother don't like hospitals. He says, "If she's not better in six hours, plenty of time for the steroids to take effect, you will need to get her checked into Bristol Regional Medical Center."

In the car I tell my father I'm worried my mother won't let me go to the hospital. He tells me not to worry. When we pull into the driveway my mother comes rushing out. "What did they say, it's nothing, isn't it?" I stand still and look to my father, who tells her it's not nothing and I should be in the hospital. "Bullshit! She doesn't need a hospital." My father tells me to go in the house and lie down, and then he lowers his voice and angrily whispers at my mother. I was prepared to be yelled at more, to be kept from getting better, but my father was a father that day, and the yelling stopped. Eventually, my mother comes and lies down next to me and goes to sleep. When I don't get better both parents take me to the hospital where my mother stays with me. I try to watch cartoons, but she makes me keep the television off. She sleeps next to my hospital bed for three days, until the IV drip of steroids and antibiotics fix my throat. I wish she would go away, would stay at home, but know she won't go anywhere. She leaves my younger siblings with Ben. She likes being out of the house. She talks to the nurses, tells them she's sick, too, only the doctors don't know what's wrong with her.

I'm also thirteen when my family upgrades from the trailer to a three-bedroom house with an unfinished basement. I find Ben sitting there at the bottom of the basement stairs, his face in his hands, and he's crying. He's crying like I haven't seen him cry in years. "What is it?" I ask. "I'm a big idiot. I'm just a big idiot!" he says, over and over. "No you're not. Why are you saying that? You're not an idiot." I awkwardly pat his shoulder and again ask him why he's saying that. He finally tells me the neighbor boy (two years younger than him) was doing his homework outside and asked Ben to help him, but he couldn't. The boy kept insisting he should know, he was grades ahead of him and he should know. But he couldn't help and ran to the basement in tears. I am angry at my parents. I want to demand they send all of us to school but don't. Though I do tell my mother why Ben's crying, hoping her guilt will make her at least think of sending all of us to school. It doesn't. "Watch your little brothers," she says, as she, with a textbook in her hand, guides Ben into her bedroom for the afternoon.

I'm almost fourteen when Seth leaves home after turning eighteen. He leaves for Texas, for the father my mother had worked so hard to keep him from. I don't know what happened there, perhaps it was too late to make things right with his father—practically a stranger. When Seth calls our house a few months after leaving, I want to yell at him, had planned on what I'd say if we spoke. I'm not sure why I'm mad because we don't like each other very much, but when I finally hear his voice over the phone my eyes burn with tears I don't understand. A few months later he returns. He was worried, he said, about the rest of us kids. He doesn't stay at our house long, our mother trying to regain control over her firstborn son, a control that will never again be complete. He moves into a motel, starts working at the Winn Dixie, meets Darla, a cashier, and they quickly become engaged. They are both nineteen when they marry each other, twenty-one when they became parents for the first time.

I'm still fourteen before Seth moves into the motel. All of us living under one roof for the last time and both my older brothers try and catch me before getting in the shower. They like to taunt me, one at the bathroom door, the other at the window. I don't know which is more susceptible, the door, or the window, so decide to throw my weight against the door while screaming to be left alone. They overpower me, walk in laughing as I try to cover my body with a t-shirt. That part of me that knows how to hate, does so with a vengeance. Later I will try to forget this and other things. Seth goes to war in Iraq and returns an addict; he divorces his wife, neglects his children, and takes to the streets. Sometimes he leaves voicemails in which he asks me for money, sometimes for a place to stay, sometimes to cry about all the bad from when we were kids, and sometimes to yell at me for not caring enough. He says, "You better fucking talk to me!" But I don't. And when Ben calls to say he misses me, I freeze, for years, unable to recall that person he used to know.

The year I'm fourteen my family only moves twice, the second time to a small farmhouse on the outskirts of Rogersville, Tennessee. This is where Ben's dog dies after getting hit by some asshole speeding down our country road. The dog had straddled half yard and half asphalt when she was struck. I go with Ben to pick up her body. I carry a sheet and try to tell him not to look, to let me go first. But she was his responsibility, and he knows it hurts me to look at suffering. She is dead, though her body convulses, so he takes his shotgun to her head. He says it is to be sure he isn't withholding mercy, but now I think he just wanted to see what his bullets could do. Still, he told me to look away before he pulled the trigger.

For my fifteenth birthday my father lets me pick out another dog from the pound. A sweet dog who turns out likes to chase cars. I work with him so he won't chase cars. It's helping, I think, to lock him in the laundry room for half an hour each time he chases a car. So for a month I train him, and I would have trained him longer, but he gets hit by a car. Probably I never should have gotten the dog. I wasn't allowed to keep him inside with me, and he had a knack for getting out of the fence. I remember caring for the animal but I can't remember his name.

I block some things out, or maybe I just forget. He gets hit by a car and I run to him, but there is no one home to take us to the vet. So I sit with my dog, hold him and touch him, and tell him he'll be alright. He laps at me, seems alright, there is only a little blood. But then he convulses, which scares me—reminding me of Ben's dog—so I beg the woman who hit him, a single mother with a screaming child inside a beat-up car, to please take us to the vet. By the time I get my dog in the car, with the help of an older man who pulled over to survey the scene, my dog is dead. I never cry, not while there is still something to be done, but when I see my dog give out a final breath and blood leak from his mouth, I do. And then the old man is taking my hand, saying something about nature, about the cycle of life. I shake off his hand and go to take my dog back out of the car. I will avoid getting another animal until I am an adult, living in Salt Lake City, and my boyfriend will present me with the small gray kitten he withdraws from his pocket. I will back away and stare at both of them, angry, my boyfriend asking me to love this tiny, shaking, feral thing.

Not too long before I leave home, my father tells me he will help me. He doesn't know how, but he will help. He wants me to have dreams that come true, though he asks if I don't think he has any dreams of his own. I wonder about them, his dreams, and think he could have done anything, gone anywhere, could have been happy, but he picked the wrong woman and never did figure out how to set it right. I don't believe my father's dreams will ever come true because there is something impossible there. I ask him again, how will he help, hopeful to put my plans of running away, of leaving the babies, on the back burner. He says he will help me get into school, but then says if I tell anyone, tell my mother, he'll say I lied and will pretend he knows nothing about the conversation. Later, when I run away, I wonder why my father made a promise he had no intention of keeping, of offering help he would never give.

I remember my little brother, Logan, getting so angry with me, but don't recall for what. I was not always a good sister, lost patience, yelled at the babies when they misbehaved. A few times I spanked them, and having done this tortures me and always will. Now I don't believe in spanking. The babies were just bored, needed more attention than I could give. And when Logan got angry, I got angry back, and when he yelled, I put my right hand on his beautiful, perfect face, thumb on one cheek, the rest of my fingers on the other, and I squeezed. Like my father always did to me; I stared in his face. I hate myself for doing something my father would have done. And the next day, when a tiny blue bruise the size of my thumbprint appears on Logan's cheek, I feel sick. It's my biggest regret. I want to tell him, tell him I'm most sorry for this, for not being better. And I do, but he doesn't remember the bruise; years later, he can't recall it.

I write a last letter to my grandmother when I'm around fifteen. She had mailed me a letter in which she asked if I had a boyfriend or wouldn't my father let me have one? I replied to her, happy to be asked. I tell her that if I fell in love, it wouldn't matter what anyone else, including my father, said. It's a silly thing to have written and I know it. I wouldn't know how to talk to a boy if I were stuck alone with one for days on end. But I've read a lot of books, some with love stories in them, and I like the romantic idea of falling in love and nothing getting in the way. So, I write this to my grandmother who I have not seen since I was twelve years old. She's my father's mother. She always had parakeets, which is what prompted me to get a pet parakeet of my own. I love my grandmother, though my mother has no fondness for her. I'm upstairs putting my little sister to bed when my mother yells for me to come downstairs. I kiss Samantha's face, tuck the blanket around her baby body, and then go to my mother. She's waving my opened letter in the air wildly, demanding to know what I was thinking by sending this filth to my grandmother. "Why did you open that?" I demand. "Because you were sneaky about it and I knew you were hiding something." I tell her I'm not hiding anything, just wanted to write my grandmother a damn letter. Probably because I don't apologize or cower, perhaps because I cussed, my mother pauses, then she says, "Punctuation. Do you even know the difference between a comma and a period?" My face gets red with embarrassment, and her lips curve in a smile.

I remember my mother scanning her face in the mirror, looking for traces of her own mother, pulling at the skin around her eyes and under her chin. She fills in the deep pink outlines around her lips with brighter pink lipstick. She goes outside with me, sits on the porch, and insists on drawing flowers—she says this activity is just as good as any science lesson I'd get from school—and draws her flower in pink and, like her lips, draws dark lines on the outsides, each petal putting up its own barrier against the next. My flowers are messy. I didn't even know what I was drawing, some kind of pansy, I think. My mother's flowers are perfectly drawn and when I ask her to show me how, she says hers is a natural gift, one that can't be taught.

I'm sixteen when Darla is pregnant with her first of two children and she invites my family over to the house she and Seth rent from her parents next door. My mother and I bring the children over to play with Darla's nephew, an exciting and unusual outing for my siblings, and, as odd as it is, I think, just for the briefest moment, that maybe things are going to be okay, that my mother will not insist on creating drama with Seth and Darla. All seems well as the children play, and my mother behaves herself, is having a "good day." Those "good days," I have begun to learn, are not to be trusted, if for no other reason than the days following always encompassed a relapse of the unknown sickness my mother claimed to have. I hated her for that feigned sickness, and I started to hate the sight of my mother's body—the way it always seemed gray, her face drooping downward. I thought she looked what she felt on the inside and I hated seeing that, too. But the day we visit Seth and Darla, she rolls her hair, brightens her face with makeup, and puts on actual clothes instead of a nightgown. I should have known this was her preparing to wage war. Part of me probably does know, but wants to be wrong, for everything to be okay. It seems safe enough to sneak out back and have a cigarette with Seth. I wash my hands at the basement sink next to the washer, chew a stick of gum Seth hands me, spray myself with perfume, then follow Seth up the stairs only to find Darla in tears. Her pregnant belling bulging from her small frame as she shakes, unable to find words. My mother's face holds a proud smirk, happy with the insults she's hurled so easily at the young mother-to-be.

Just after my seventeenth birthday, my mother returns to the house from the psychiatric ward of the hospital in Abingdon or Elizabethton, I'm not sure which. She stays in bed all day. Her presence stifles the calm of her absence. It had been easier for me to tend the babies without her around. They were at ease and so was I. Her presence exacerbates my feelings that things are not going to improve. I attempt a stay against these feelings, but fail. I pick up the phone, which I should have picked up years ago but was too scared, my parents made me too scared, and called the superintendent of schools. If the cops were going to show up and take me and the babies away, then so be it. No cops show up. No truant officer shows up—maybe because I didn't give them enough information, maybe because in Rogersville, Tennessee, no one really gives a fuck. But my mother, who was supposed to be sleeping, had been listening to my every move, heard when I softly picked up the phone, stepped into the laundry room, and made the call. And then I feel her rage, pathetic, inarticulate rage, in which she follows me down the sidewalk and yells at me for the call. Yells at me in front of the babies, in front of Ben who had just pulled up the drive, in front of the neighbors. And I turn around and tell her it's right, what I did, it was right because the kids should be in school. She stays in her robe. Yells for the children to gather in the prayer room, will not let me near them, locks me out of the house for a while, until the children get rambunctious. Then she locks all of us out of the house together. My father will return from work, will not yell at me, but will remind me behind the closed door of the prayer room, a door which my mother beats upon and demands to be let in, that my phone call could have separated the family forever. The babies don't understand all the yelling, don't understand why I would do something to separate the family.

After I run away to Indiana, I study. I make friends who help me study. At eighteen I take the GED and then the SATs, and finally I meet with the director of admissions at the local college. I tell her my SAT math scores are twenty points too low, but then explain how, even though I've been kept from attending school most of my life, I've been working, and ask if there isn't any way she could let me take classes anyway. She stares at me for a moment, me in my borrowed dress and lipstick. She tells me to wait as she fetches the director of the financial aid office. She tells me to repeat my story, so I do. Both women stare at me and then each other. Finally, the admissions director says she's admitting me, and the other woman tells me she's going to help with my financial aid paperwork. I can start college right on time. It was most important to me—to start on time. But I am not prepared for school, for the shiny floors and bright lights. I don't understand how it all works. My English instructor takes time with me, looks over my assignments in all my classes, and explains what's expected of me. A year later I will transfer schools, will move to Salt Lake City, and then earn a degree at the University of Utah. I will remember the women in Indiana and be thankful. The haze around understanding and learning slowly dissipates, but always I will play at catch-up.

For as long as I can remember, from childhood to young adulthood, my parents, mostly my mother, would insist on going for drives in the Blue Ridge Mountains. In later years the drives came out of fights between my parents—running away from one another or making up after the running away—and sometimes they would just get the itch to drive. I mostly hated those long drives, though I didn't always. I'm not sure when they got stressful, probably when the babies arrived. It was hard to keep them quiet in the car. I remember the heat, the smell of teething gel, unwanted warm bottles the baby would reject with a violent toss across the back seat. Later I'll visit a man I knew from when I lived in Utah who has moved to North Carolina and he'll want to take a drive and I won't want to go, will try to show rather than saying outright that I don't want to, but will go anyway. He'll drive by places that will make me ache for the desert, for the Cottonwood Canyons, for the thin mountain air back home. I'll feel resentful of being back in the Blue Ridge Mountains of my childhood, but I'll fight the feeling and I'll never tell him. After the visit I call things off and he is surprised. I'll recall that fucking drive and wonder why the hell I didn't scream in resistance, why I chose to please rather than disappoint.

When I am twenty-one I need a job. I find one with a river company in Marble Canyon, Arizona. I learn how to appreciate shade, how to rig boats, and, eventually, how to read water. But before I'm allowed to run the river, I work around the warehouse. My boss teaches me how to repair the spring-fed water line, and his wife tells me how to fend off the loneliness that can come from living in a vast space so beautiful it can hurt to look upon it. Years later I'll try to stop a stranger from dying in that space, his body broken on the side of the road, a car accident on 89A, just a few miles from the warehouse, but his final breath will escape while I grasp his hand, still asking him to hold on.

When I'm twenty-seven I have a temper that has gotten worse with age. It's a temper that takes time to trigger and then lose, but when it reaches just the perfect heat, I see red. I fight with my boyfriend, the one who presented me with a kitten, the one who isn't really my boyfriend anymore. I go to his place to gather up my things, he knows I'm there, though he never admits this. It's dark outside and from his living room window I watch the city lights flicker across the valley, Kennecott Mine somewhere in the distance, a massive hole where a mountain once stood—I try to locate it in the darkness, but can't. He walks in with another woman and in an instant I am not me, but a violent version of me. This woman is larger than me, yet it's easy to pick her up and set her out of the apartment when she refuses to leave. And Jonah, my not boyfriend, yells at me, says he could be "mid-fuck" right now. I punch him in the head before he says this, and after the words leave his mouth, I go to walk out the door. He blocks it, insists I sit down. And I do, feeling the heat leave my body as he reminds me of all my walls. My skin is pink and clammy, sweat sticks to the hair around my face, and I notice I'm breathing hard as I stare at this man who sits across from me with his hands on my knees. And I think that most of this is my fault because I don't know how to love right.

When I'm twenty-nine I move to Missouri, leaving behind the mountains and the desert, the west, the home I made my own. This flatland will bring me to the ground, cover me in a humid blanket so thick I have to remind myself to breathe. I'll walk through the small downtown of Columbia, Missouri and wonder if maybe I should have stopped to see if all this education was still what I wanted. I'll go home in the summer, Utah and Arizona, and my river people will tease about moving to "Misery," and we will all laugh, cold beer in hand after a day of rigging, preparing boats for another trip down the Grand. But I know I'm beaten down and so does my boss, who says he's worried. I look out at the Vermilion cliffs—cast like giants against a setting sun, drink one last beer for the night, smoke a last cigarette, and finally tell my boss it worries me that he worries.

End of Ballet

Before college, before the river, before leaving Tennessee, when I'm just a few months past my fifteenth birthday, I stand outside of the dressing room door in a local high school theatre and I light the stick of incense I bought with change from a gas station. I watch the smoke rise and curl in the air and tell myself it's for good luck. The white tulle layered around my legs feels like a shield of peace, of protection maybe. In the dressing room girls are giggling as they fasten each other up, placing last minute pins in their hair and extra coats of lipstick on already deep red lips. Staring at the incense makes my eyes water. I drop the stick on the cement floor, stand on it and watch it smolder beneath my pointe shoe. It's the last day of performance week and I feel sickening disappointment in my gut every time I remember I have to return home after the last act. *La Sylphide*, act two, ethereal and deathly romantic. A man kills the girl of his dreams by accident, and the ghosts of women try to claim his life in retaliation. I love this act, the music, a perfect combination of beauty and sadness. I listen to the notes, the sound filling the theatre, and I mold to my shoes as they and my skin bake beneath the hot stage lights. The concrete hallways beneath the stage are a haven, and when I'm hidden in the long black curtains that make up the wings, I understand I'm in the only safe darkness I know. And that was important, that bit of safety, that small bit of calm. Ballet—music and the movement, the tulle and make-up—transformed me. When I pulled on a leotard, slipped on a pointe shoe, and pinned my hair back, I was not the self I was at home—caregiver and tired. I was, for a few hours, able to understand what it might be like to be my own person, to have agency, to be someone my mother was trying so hard to keep me from being. This glimpse of a self I might be, revealed through ballet, snuck up on me over the years. I had never wanted to be a dancer. And though my mother pushed me into classes with the hope that it might transform me, make me less like the boys she already had, a professional ballet dancer was the last thing she wanted me to be. Eventually, she realized the dancing had not transformed me into the girl she envisioned. So ballet became a thing that displeased her, especially when I came to love it. My mother was resentful of the world it threatened to open up for me. And so ballet became the thing she used against me—always threatening to take it away, following through with those threats for months at a time, saying it was too expensive, even though my teacher had stopped charging tuition so I could keep training and another teacher kept me in new shoes and tights.

After my final performance I gingerly hang up my tutu, touch the tulle then the satin bodice—soft against my working hands. I pull myself away and leave the theatre as people, mostly families of the other dancers, gather for a celebratory reception. I walk outside and approach the van parked at the theatre's entrance. Ben is in the driver's seat, and my mother is talking to him with a smile on her face, and they are waiting to take me back to Rogersville, Tennessee—the town forty-five minutes away that we'd just moved to a few months before. As soon as I open the and door climb in, she turns to look at me, her face covered in layers of pink blush and lipstick, her eyelashes coated in mascara and lids overdone in gray-blue eye shadow.

"Well, that didn't make any sense at all."

"What didn't?"

"The ballet."

"What didn't make sense about it?"

"For starters, all those ghosts in the woods with that man, who by the way, is a homosexual and disgusting."

"I don't think he's disgusting."

"It doesn't really matter what you think. God's the judge. And God has told me you're not to dance anymore, not for a long time. I've already told your teacher you won't finish out the year."

I lean back, close my eyes, and say nothing.

At home the house is a disaster on top of being dirty. My father has been ripping rooms apart to remodel them. All the children are now sleeping in one room, beds are piled between the four short walls like sardines, and children's clothes and toys are strung across the floor. I crawl under a blanket in the nearest bed. It smells like piss. I get up and move to another bed. I fall asleep. My mother sends Ben in to tell me to go to the kitchen. I pretend not to hear him, but when he starts to step toward the bed I jump up and move quick. I find both parents sitting at the table and immediately know what this signals. I have my mother's speech memorized. "You have strayed from God and your family, and so we have decided you can't go to ballet for some time . . ." When she starts the speech I cut her off.

"I know, I know. I'm not allowed to finish the year. I don't need to hear this again."

"Well, this time you aren't going back for a long time. You aren't stepping into that studio for *at least* a year, if ever again," my mother says.

I tear up, which seems to satisfy her, perhaps because I so rarely let her see me cry, and a familiar smile spreads across her face. My father, as usual, says nothing. I look at him, but he won't make eye contact.

"Don't look at him for help. He's just as fed up with you as I am."

I say nothing as my parents get up to run errands, leaving me to make dinner for the babies. I stare into the cupboards a few moments. Noah pops his head through the kitchen doorway and grins at me with a nearly toothless mouth.

"You lost another tooth!" I say.

"Yep," he giggles.

"Tooth Fairy bring you anything?"

"Mom says the Tooth Fairy is a lie."

"That's pathetic," I say under my breath, wishing I'd been around to leave a little treasure beneath his pillow.

For dinner I make refried bean and cheese burritos. Afterwards I go to the bathroom—examine the blisters my pointe shoes left on my first and second toes, and then I pop open my mother's painkillers and attempt an overdose because I am tired, and more than that, I'm tired of being tired.

Prism

The pills did not kill me, and likely would have only made me sick had I been left alone, though they did make it difficult to walk, to use my hands. It was my stumbling about while cleaning up the dinner I made that night that prompted my mother to taunt me for not standing up straight: "I thought ballet dancers walked with a stick up their behind all the time," she had said, accusing me of throwing a fit, my bent body a statement of rebellion. Ben laughed at first, but then something told him to check the medicine cabinet. That was all it took. My mother yells like an insane person, finds my father, and both of them drive me to the emergency room, furious.

The doctor who pumps my stomach tells them that he's legally obligated to report this, and if they are smart they will admit me to a hospital in Knoxville. Everyone in the emergency room I interact with talks to me like I'm trying for attention, someone says as much to my parents, mostly responding to my mother who keeps repeating I'm just throwing a fit. All the same, I'm sent to the hospital in Knoxville for three days. There, I feel my depression lighten as I'm allowed to read and sleep, and eat, and I only have to talk a little.

When my parents insist on checking me out before the doctor has authorized my release, I know it's because they want me back to tend the children, but I say nothing of this to anyone. I say nothing at all other than I want to go to school. The doctor says my parents have not been helpful, tells me to stay strong and set goals for myself. A social worker gives me a number and tells me where to go if I ever feel unsafe. I never use the number and I never feel safe.

By the time I'm nearly sixteen and still living in Rogersville, Tennessee, I'm shucking tobacco in work boots, and ballet shoes seem something of another world. Lenny, the farmer I sometimes work for, has a daughter, Lucy, who had dreams for herself, who wanted to live, but was killed not a year after I attempted to take my own life. I imagine what it would have been like for Lenny the day he found his girl, the flesh of his flesh, distorted and cold. He's looking for Lucy, who hadn't come home last night. He scans his land—the cows and tobacco fields—a second job to his first as a CNC machinist, the kind of factory worker who monitors machines, made of metal, cut metal. He is a quiet man, tall, with a long dark beard, not too short brown hair, clear blue-gray eyes, a gentle voice. This Tennessee winter day is not so unlike any other—the cold coaxing frost to lie thick on dead leaves that cover wilted grass with their damp weight, and trees stand like bony structures against the early morning sky. The heat of Lenny's boots melts the frost, leaving behind his footprints, marking a clear trail from the front door of his home to his truck. He has an uneasy feeling as he jiggles his keys in his pocket, removes them, and, just before he unlocks the pickup, notices Lucy's car not too far in the distance. He puts the keys back in his pocket and sets off toward the car, picking up speed when he sees the silhouette of her body in the driver's seat. The driver's side window is shattered, fragments of glass are strewn about and the rising sun reflects brilliantly from each tiny piece. She is pale, and there is no movement, no trace of breath. Still, Lenny holds his own breath so that he might hear hers, reaches for her wrist—hopeful for a pulse.

"Lucy, can you hear me?" he asks.

No response. He stares at his girl, becomes fixated on her lifeless hands. He takes off his coat and wraps it around her body.

Ben works in the tobacco fields in the spring and summer, but not in the autumn after the tobacco stalks are pierced and hung to dry for months. He returns to the job in the winter, when brisk air lingers in bones and stiffens the earth, and the tobacco stalks are pulled down and shucked, the darkened leaves divided into separate piles according to their grade. Working tobacco is a second job, one Ben goes to only when he feels like it or wants the extra money. I think he uses cash to buy junk food and tobacco on his way to Cherokee Lake for fishing when the water is high or for mudding when the waters are drained for winter.

Lenny's an easy employer and tells Ben that if I'm interested, he'll hire me, too. Though I've never touched any part of a tobacco plant, outside of the cigarettes I've stolen now and then, I want money, and I want out of the house and all the work that comes with it. At first our mother says I can't go, says she needs me at home, but I plead with her and Ben insists he doesn't want to work on the farm without me, so eventually she allows me to go, but only now and then and only for a few hours at a time. She doesn't like to be left alone with my four little brothers and sister.

I've seen the drag on Saturday nights in downtown Rogersville. People my age gather in cars and drive slow and steady down Main Street, turn by the Hardees, and either make the block or pull over and make out in the Food City parking lot. Nobody seems unhappy—silly maybe, or bored. My father says they are all just wasting gas to show off their cars. My mother says the drag is a sin, full of sinful people, and things happen to sinful people. I'm not jealous of the kids on the drag, but curious. I wouldn't know what to say if a boy asked me into his car, wouldn't know how to talk because my speak is from a world he wouldn't be able to understand any more than I could understand his.

Later, after meeting Lenny, I'll wonder if his daughter met her boyfriend, Todd, at the drag. If he, being just too old for high school, rode the drag and looked for girls that might let him fog up the windows. Then I'll think of what it would be like to be pregnant in high school. Then I'll just wonder about high school; after all, I already know what pregnancy looks like. It's weirdly funny, to feel dread at the sight of a positive pregnancy test not my own, secretly hoping that my mother will miscarry because the thought of tending to another child is exhausting. I wonder if Lucy wished that on herself, to fall down the stairs or something—anything to get rid of the thing growing inside her. That's what I'd have done: starved myself and then thrown my body down some stairs for good measure. But Lucy didn't do any of those things. She became a mother and went on living. I wonder if she ever regretted her choice, or if, when she looked at her daughter, her heart hurt out of too much love.

Bundled up in a thick flannel shirt, dark green coat, blue jeans, and the new pair of boots Ben bought me, I wipe at my dripping nose with my sleeve. It's just a bit after five in the morning and I stay out of sight by sitting on the cold concrete steps of our back porch. *No way Mom will come outside this early*, I think. It's still dark outside—not even pink hints of light have snuck over the hills. My ears are fine-tuned for sounds that could wake the children and, knowing that all of my younger siblings are early risers and not very sound sleepers, I wish Ben would hurry up. Every noise causes me to catch my breath as I listen for the sounds of Samantha's cry or one of the boys' small but quick paced steps. Finally, the soft creak of the screen door is followed by the sound of Ben's footsteps.

"Cold out here," he whispers.

"Not too bad," I reply.

"Boots good?" he asks.

"Uh huh. Thanks. I'll pay you back," I say.

"Don't worry about it, Rachel. You gotta have new shoes every once in a while. Besides, those were cheap."

I wonder if this—the perfect new work boots, along with the help getting out of the house (he's never given a shit about working alone)—is Ben's attempt to say he's sorry. I don't bother to ask: instead I follow him to the car and stay quiet as we drive toward the farm.

As a teenager Ben is the good one, which may be why he mostly passes under the radar of my parents' overly watchful eyes. So when my father once yelled at Ben instead of me, I didn't know what to do with myself. I snuck out my bedroom window and sat on the faded green tin roof with my knees pulled underneath my chin. Ben came up the stairs after my father stopped hollering while my mother watched on approvingly—always approving of anyone's shame but her own. He called out my name in a harsh whisper, "Rachel! Where did you go?"

I poked my head through the window and said, "I can't believe that was you and not me down there for once."

He laughed, said it wouldn't last. And he was right; it wouldn't. Then we jumped off the roof, his knee coming up against his lip hard, drawing blood, but still we ran fast. Our father stormed out the front door and yelled but didn't make to catch us. We went down to Lakeshore Market and bought candy, then we went to the lake bottom and scanned the mud. I looked at my brother as he threw rocks across the dried-up lake bed and thought about how I stayed awake at night until he fell asleep. Though it only happened once, I'll never forgive him for causing me to lurch awake to shove off his hands that were trying to know my fourteen-year-old body.

Fuck him for reminding me there was no safe space under my parents' roof, I think as I look at him now, driving with a stern look, his eyes with the same muted purple beneath them that he's had since he was a child. It's confusing though because I still love the child him. The brother everyone thought was my twin when we were younger, the boy who could throw a baseball better than any kid his age, who always took the fish off the hook so I didn't have to, who loved candy more than any person I'd ever known. And then I hate part of this grown up him who made me a target inside a house where I was defined only by my sex.

The way my mother demanded modesty made me feel as if being a girl were my fault, as if my body made me a sinner before I even figured out exactly what sin was. She would make me model my clothes in front of my father while my brothers looked on in the background. It wasn't that my father cared all that much about what I wore; he was quiet on most subjects and let my mother go about her business. Let her strike the kids for no reason or lock herself up in her room for days on end. She said she prayed. And I suspect she did pray, sometimes getting the answers she wanted between burning herself with cigarettes and sleeping the day away. Sometimes, she'd show us those perfectly round burns on her wrists and ankles. I used to try and break into her bedroom when I smelled the smoke, to prevent her from putting hot ash against her soft flesh, but after a while I stopped caring. Later, after I got out of that house, I heard she set her bedroom on fire. It was said to be an accident, but I knew better. She'd left a candle burning next to lace curtains, while my little siblings, all of them under ten years old, sat in that house alone. Maybe I was too ready to think the worst of my mother, but there was something about that fire, something about her, that made me think she set it on purpose.

It's a strange thing, to love and hate my brother like this—it's something I can't make sense of. So I stare out the windows, at the hills rolling everywhere around me—all dried up and yellow. If I didn't know any better, I'd think the earth was choking to death in the chill of a snowless winter.

At Lenny's farm I quickly learn not to touch my eyes after handling the tobacco because it intensely burns them, especially when the plant is still green. I won't discover the difference between the green and brownish-red plants until summertime, when the green stalks grow up out of the ground in humid fields. The sting of sweat will slide into my eyes and make them run like the eyes of a child smarting from the sting of a switch across bare legs or from a mother's perfectly aimed slap.

Lenny has put together a small crew to shuck his tobacco: Todd, Lenny Jr., Ben, and me. Not much is said among the five of us because Ben's naturally shy, and I'm not used to being out of the house or interacting with people outside of my family since we moved to Rogersville about a year ago. As for the others, well, I just assume they aren't big talkers. But then, Lenny mentions deer hunting and each man quickly picks up the speak of bucks, bows, tree stands, rifles, and deer piss.

The methodic rhythm of ripping leaf after leaf from stalk after stalk has a way of slowing time, and as the hunting talk picks up, my mind wanders, and I notice that if I squint just right, I can see the sunlight peeking through the cracks between the long planks of wood that make up the shaky barn walls, the pathetic barrier between one sad place and another. Somewhere, beyond those hills, deer are trying to get fat for the fawns they carry. I wonder if they move slower when they're pregnant or if, when a hunter is shameful enough to kill after the rut, he ever notices signs of a swollen belly or pieces of a would-be fawn mingled in with the entrails and guts he removes from her body. I suppose the fawn is better off dead, anyway. Too many deer in these hills—she'd probably starve to death if a hunter didn't get her.

I like to think of Lenny as a kind hunter, the sort of man who took his boy and girl out in the woods as soon as they were old enough and taught them what he knew: the way to stay quiet, never to shoot a deer with white spots of youth or a swollen gut, always to aim to kill, and, if for some reason the first shot isn't fatal, always to be quick to fire another. Never to let a creature suffer. "Don't waste what nature gives you," he'd say, as he knelt down with a blade, showing his children how to gut the animal.

By the time I've worked for a few weeks, both in the morning and evening hours, I get comfortable enough around Lenny to look him in the eye instead of at the ground when he offers a friendly hello. He's kind to me, always gentle when he speaks. He offers that he grew up in Rogersville and asks how I like the place. I'm honest when I say I wish we still lived in Kingsport, because there I'd been able to train in ballet, the only thing that ever got me out of the house. He understands how it might be hard to give up that for working on a tobacco farm. I agree, but don't tell him so, and instead tell him how the work is good, how it lets me save up for going someplace else. Ben is quiet when I say this to Lenny, perhaps because he knows the money won't get me far.

I like listening to Lenny and Lenny Jr. speak of Lucy and her daughter, Leah. In a way I'm almost envious of Lucy—not of her child, and certainly not of her boyfriend, but of her freedom to come and go from her house as she pleases, and of the love her father so clearly has for her. Had he always loved this way? How was it, when Lucy looked at him and confessed Todd had got her pregnant? Was his voice still calm and gentle? Did she cry? Did she say right away she was going to keep it? Did he worry more about money, about the new mouth to feed, body to clothe, love to give? Did she ask him to help, or did she know he would never make her ask?

Todd tends to speak up a bit more when Lenny isn't around, but I stay cold-faced and quiet around him. It isn't that I have any idea that he will eventually murder Lucy when she attempts to leave him. It's not as if I look at him and see a killer, though his violent acts will not surprise me. But that doesn't mean much because, for the most part, I wouldn't be surprised by any man's violence. After Todd's crime, I'll picture his round face screwed up in anger, turning red, making his blond hair appear lighter, as he wraps a chubby finger around the trigger. But for now, it's simply the way Todd speaks to me that grates on my nerves, and I prefer the maddening but softer sound of working the tobacco to his voice. The quiet doesn't last, though; silence is not something Todd seems comfortable with, and it doesn't take him long to strike up a conversation.

"Kind of dainty to be out here, aren't ya? What are you, fourteen?" Todd asks, looking at me.

"Fifteen, and I'm working just as good as you," I say, tossing aside yet another freshly shucked stalk.

"So. You used to be a ballet dancer," he says, ignoring my response.

"Still am," I say. "Just have to take some time off, that's all."

"Time off, my ass!" Ben says.

I glare at Ben, toss a half-shucked plant to the floor, and then turn to leave. I walk the distance from the barn to a pile of remnants that, at one time, was some kind of shed. I walk away because I know Ben's right; I know it's not simply a break. My mother might call it a break, but the truth is she has no intention of letting me return to the studio. I huddle down behind the broken planks and cracked foundation to light a stolen cigarette. The wind is picking up—stings my nose and eyes with its icy whip, cutting and sharp. I shut my eyes to protect them from the wind and attempt to hold back tears that have nothing to do with the cold. I get closer to the ground and feel the wet mud dampen the rear end of my pants. The sun has long been hidden by the shades of an overcast sky and the hills feel more lonely than ever—vast and unyielding. I try to remember the perfect heat of stage lights and how they had a way of baking my skin and warming every part of me perfectly. And the music, how the notes pushed their sound around corners, through walls, and over the theatre's thick velvet curtains. Then comes a long note, subtle, soft. It fills my ears; it's the wind picking up momentum, slipping over hills and through slumbering tree limbs. It is the sound of right now, and it is not for me, but it is on me, around me, over me, through me, cold and unforgiving. Slowly, the wind's sound brings me back to the dampness, to the now that pushes against my longing, that hurt for something lost and desire for something better, that need for something better, and is forcefully replacing it with a reality that demands submission and numbness.

I again find myself wondering about Lucy, whether she feels anything like what I feel or if she is happy with her life, happy with Todd. Out of shape, flattop-wearing, mustache-sporting, always-dropping-nasty-comments-about-sex Todd. Mostly I ignore him. What is there to say? He has his ways. Still, I can't help but imagine Lucy is with Todd because she doesn't know what else to do. Though wouldn't her dad help? Lenny can't stand to see suffering. Maybe the love that was once between Lucy and Todd has dissipated and she doesn't yet know how to walk away from her child's father. The truth is that outside of what her father and brother say about her, I don't know much of anything about Lucy, having only ever seen her walking out of the house to her car, a smallish figure, as the house sits a good half-mile from the barn. I've only been able to make out her long black hair, which, even from a distance, looks beautiful and wavy. Lucy's only about three years older than me, but that doesn't mean much. She has a kid—something that separates her from me.

I walk back to the barn, pick up the stalk I'd thrown on the ground, and begin to remove its leaves. When I look up from my work, Todd is staring off through the door, shucking the tobacco quickly and with precision. Ben is looking right at me and says, "Well, we better get you home before Mom gets upset."

I don't say anything as I remove my gloves, black with the sticky residue from the tobacco, and make my way to the Chevy.

A few days later I dress myself for the cold hours ahead in the barn. I get to spend the whole morning working because it's

Saturday, and for once my father is going to stay home and help look after the kids. When I walk into the kitchen, Ben tells me we aren't going.

"Why not," I ask, unable to hide the disappointment in my voice.

"I just got off the phone with Lenny. He says Lucy's dead."

"She is not, don't say shit like that!"

"Yeah, she is. Todd shot her two days ago. Lenny said they've been fighting about her moving to Knoxville. She was leaving him."

"Serious?"

"Serious."

I lean against the stove, stare at my boots, and wonder what will become of Leah, now the child of a dead mother and a murdering father.

I read over Lucy's obituary many times before her funeral and then find myself reading the other obituaries in the paper, surprised to find no accidents, no unexplained death of a youth, and no illness that comes outside of old age. It's a small town and calm deaths are to be expected, too. The obituaries all sound the same, or at least nearly the same. Lucy's stands out only because she is so young, the youngest death in the paper by a few decades. Most of the other people had lived their whole lives in Rogersville, Tennessee. Most of them left behind generations that would also grow old and die in Rogersville.

Lucy lays in an oak coffin and her head seems sunken, as if something is missing, and this makes sense because something is missing—a large portion of her skull, all those pieces of bone and brain that had been blown off and out, spread in and around her car like bloody confetti. Yet despite her misshapen skull, her hair still looks as beautiful as ever, lying in thick dark curls around her face. I guess her eyes had been blue, like Lenny Jr.'s, only now, red surrounds that blue of his. He has cried for days, but in a silent kind of way. The whole family has a way of being silent, and then not silent at all. Lucy's mother, a woman I've never seen and had heard very little of, has a wet face, and the way she looks up at people paying their condolences has the expression of a question, but no one can offer her any answers. There are only sad and sympathetic looks and mumbled apologies, and still, she keeps looking, keeps asking. But it is Lenny's appearance that is most shocking. He wears the look of a beaten man, all sadness and wounds. His shoulders are bent, his face sunken; dark circles offset the grey blueness of his eyes, and even his beard seems to droop with the weight of his loss.

Ben and I take a seat at the back of the church. Red carpet covers the floor. The wooden pews are cushioned in the same color of red, and the lights are a severe yellow.

"I can't believe that piece of shit! I just don't know how he could have done it," Ben whispers.

I don't say anything back; instead I keep staring at the velvet dress that covers Lucy's body. I'm not surprised. Todd had it in him, after all—she was leaving him for something different, something better, somewhere better. He couldn't have that, couldn't let her have that, couldn't let her be more than what he wanted her to be. So he, surrounded by a southern landscape already too familiar with tragedy, put a shotgun against the pristine glass of her car window and pulled the trigger.

On the way back from the funeral Ben and I stop by Lakeshore Market, the small place that serves as a gas station, grocery store, bait shop, and deer weighing station. We take our time meandering through the aisles before settling on our candy and sodas, which Ben takes to the register to purchase. I fixate on the cracks running through the smooth concrete floor, noticing the dampness that seems to be seeping up through the thin spaces, the musty smell coming from the dank water, the open minnow tanks, the dark soil full of night crawlers. Through the window I notice a hunter pulling a deer carcass from the back of his truck and placing it, not too gently, onto the scales. I go outside and watch the hunter smile and say to another:

"Yeah, she's not much to be proud of, little thin, but she'll make some nice jerky and ground meat."

The tip of the deer's tongue sticks out the side of her mouth, pink and swollen, her brown eyes glassy and dull, and a bit of blood oozes from a small hole in her side. I hope the bullet ended her life quickly, painlessly.

Father

The kindness Lenny showed his family, even in his grief, made me think of my own father. At first I tried comparing the two fathers, but that didn't work out because while Lenny was broken, he never said anything about how he should have kept his daughter inside, away from the world, the way my father spoke about me. I don't think my father had always thought that way because when I was little he hadn't paid all that much attention to what I was doing out and about in our yard or in the nearby woods and creeks. Somewhere along the way something changed, but I can't place it on one particular event. I supposed his way of looking at things progressed over time.

I remember how when I was little and we still lived in Texas, my older brothers and I split our time between our great-grandparents and parents—there would be days on days when I wouldn't see my father at all. But there is one day when we are with our mother and she's packing us into the semitruck our father drives across the state. He's gone off route to pick us up. Night falls shortly but the darkness isn't complete, is lit in yellow and red—car lights speckled all around and as far as I can see in the distance. Ben and I pull my red and white blanket with its cotton frilly border, ripped slightly at a corner, as close to our bodies as we can. Seth sits on the floor and complains about the heat coming from underneath him. That's when my mother, who is doing the driving now, sends me to the sleeping quarters in the back of the cabin hidden from view by thick black drapes—so Seth can share the seat with Ben. I'd been cold despite being tucked closed to Ben, both of us trembling slightly because the blanket was not quite big enough. It didn't matter—I wanted to be near my brothers and the cold was worth that nearness. Still, I obeyed my mother and went to the sleeper and lay down next to my father. I fidgeted against his arms wrapped around me and cried for Ben. I remember not even trying to restrain my tears. My father had been kind, tried to coo me to sleep—I must have been around three, and I did not take to being settled, didn't like my father for trying to settle me. I cried until I got my way, got back near Ben, though that meant sitting on the hot floor—it was my turn to be there. It smelled of oil and rubber, left dark streaks on my skin but I didn't care. Later, though, when I'd grown some and my father stayed behind in Texas to work for nine months when the rest of us moved to Tennessee, I'd remember pushing my father away that day in the semitruck and feel bad about it.

As an adult, I sometimes search for moments in which my father had been kind. I'm not sure why I do this—part of me is fine not understanding him, the other part still wants some clarity. That's difficult, though, because, unlike my mother, who my father is has never been clear to me. People, it seemed, always preferred my father over my mother. I think he must have been friendly, made jokes, was better socially than her. He might have been quieter; his crazy didn't reveal itself the way my mother's did. But I'm not sure if that means all that much.

When we still lived in Texas and I was about four years old, I found a kitten and begged my father to help me with her because she was hot and flies swarmed the poor thing, and there were fleas blackening her yellow fur. My father put some eyewash in the kitten's eyes, then made me put her back where I found her. The animal died. My father's carelessness with that animal seems now to capture the same carelessness he had with his own children. It's not as simple as that, though, not really, but it's the idea of doing something for show and telling himself that was enough. A duty fulfilled, like dousing a kitten's eyes with old eyewash he pulled out of his toolbox in the trunk of his car, then insisting his four-year-old daughter return the animal to the crumbling shed from which she came. I suppose he thought that was better than nothing, that after all he could have done nothing. My father's way of doing things for show would mean something to me for a while, for years even, until I finally understood it for what it was.

In the heat of one Texas summer, I run away on Ben's bike that's too big for me. I tell my father before going, and he says he hopes I'll enjoy myself. I crash the bike. Too embarrassed to show how the crash hurt, and too stubborn to give up leaving home, I walk down the road and hide in a ditch. It is Ben who brings me back before dark, but it's my father who washes the road rash on my elbow, puts hydrogen peroxide on the broken skin, asks me if I plan on running away again soon. I shrug, try to hide how pleased I am to have him tend my hurt.

My father gave up being a semitruck driver before I was five, finally landing a job in a factory. He'd work in factories or be laid off from factories for the rest of my childhood. At one point, he worked for a factory that built things for Desert Storm—he'd seem pleased to be working a job that helped with the war. I remember a t-shirt he wore with cartoon bombs landing on Iraqis. American soldiers in fatigues, Iraqis in sandaled feet and robes. I didn't understand it—but he pointed it out to us with pride the first time he came home with it. Before that factory had laid him off, the job that made it possible for him to join us in Tennessee, he worked at Texas Instruments. I don't remember where he worked next, but the last job he had while I was still living with my family was Dodge. In that factory he was a CNC machinist. He met a woman there and they had an affair—I know because she called looking for him in the middle of the night once. Most of his shifts were night shifts or second shifts, rarely did he work days. He'd come home sleepy in the morning, and us kids would see him briefly before he'd go to bed. In the afternoon he'd wake, shower, leave. Before working at Dodge, before things were the most unbearable, my mother would leave with him before his shift began. Sometimes, on his days off, they would be gone for most of the day. Those were the days when we'd rifle for change in couch cushions and our father's dirty jean pockets to buy food at the nearest gas station.

When my father finally joined us in Tennessee, we lived in a one-bedroom apartment on "The Property," called so by the church that was situated on rolling acres of land. The church had built a school, apartments, houses, a small park. It was here that I would go to kindergarten, where I would learn how to read, and where we lived when my great-grandfather died back in Texas. My mother had moved us here for Bible school, so she said, but in reality her biggest motivator, I would learn as a teenager, was that she trying to keep Seth from his real father. It was in this apartment where my parents would tell us how my father finally came to accept Jesus, and we would gather on the floor to pray. Even as a young child the intimacy of praying and weeping made me uncomfortable—perhaps it was the heat of our five bodies so close in the living room. I don't recall how the tears came, but my father, our mother tells us, was sad for so long because he was adopted and his father was not a kind man. My father tells us he will not abandon his family the way his own father did. Now, as an adult, I know there are different ways of abandonment, different ways of being present and not present.

The period of my childhood in which my family is homeless we drive across the country. My father looks for work; my mother negotiates with different churches she wants to visit for places to stay. Every new stopover comes with a fresh act of charity I find humiliating. My father drives us all the way to Colorado, even though there are no job prospects. This is where he wishes we could live. The Rockies. He loves the Rockies. We stay at a YMCA for two days. On one of those two nights my father takes us kids to the YMCA cafeteria, though he refuses to buy himself a meal. He tells the café worker, an elderly woman, about the tough times he's come upon—I hear him start in on his struggle to find work, which prompts me to move away from him quickly, my face burning with shame. I am too embarrassed to eat the food, to show my hunger. When my father joins us at the table he tells us to be quick so we can get back to our mother, who is waiting in the room. Before we leave, the café woman comes to our table and sets down a few to-go containers filled with food—my father makes a show of protest, but she shushes him with a wave of her hand and a stern look. So he smiles, takes up the boxes, and us kids follow him out the door. Back in the hotel room, he shares the story of his luck and free food with our mother. The boxes are left on the tiny table near a window looking out on trees I don't recognize. I'm staring at these trees while my father and mother say something to us kids about staying put, then they leave and go to dinner away from the YMCA. After they leave, I walk to the boxes of food and eat with ease, far away from eyes that would see my hunger and feel pity.

After a few days in Colorado we head to Texas, where we stay for a month or two, I can't recall exactly how long. And then we end up back in Tennessee. I remember, throughout all those nights driving, when city lights woke me up and seemed to offer something I didn't quite understand, I sat up, pushing my face between the two front seats of our Ford van to get a better glimpse. My father would motion for me to be quiet, but let me sit up as long as I wanted.

When I tried to end my life the day of my last ballet performance in Kingsport—that first night in the hospital my father cried, actual tears that drove him to give me a quick hug and leave my hospital room. It had surprised me because he'd been so angry up until then. My mother stayed angry with me, though, and grew more so for making my father cry: "Look what you have done." And later, once my parents removed me from the hospital after ignoring the doctor's orders, I'd sit nearly unmovable on the floor of the room I shared with my baby sister while my father, far from tears, yelled so loud it felt as though the room shook. He threatened to send me to a juvenile jail and never let me see my siblings again. Though his anger wouldn't stop the weight pressing down on my chest, it did send a shock of fear or pain or both through my body, and I suppose that's one way of breaking up the monotony of depression. I stood up then, not because I was afraid of being sent away—that would have been a relief—but because I couldn't take the thought of being away from my siblings. So I collected my crying sister from her crib and told me father to stop yelling, to look, I was okay and I could take care of the baby now. He quieted then, though his face still fumed red, his dark brows furrowed in anger. My mother told me to leave the room and I did, sinking back to the floor with my sister in my arms as soon as I was out of eyesight of my parents. As I sat there I told myself over and over to be alright. I'd have to make a show of being okay until I was because I could not leave the babies behind.

Right around the time I turned seventeen, my father told me how hard it was for him to stay, and I remember thinking if only he would divorce my mother and take us with him, there could still be a way for me to stay close to my siblings. He was having his affair with the woman from the Dodge factory where they worked together, so maybe that prompted his confession of wanting to leave. He didn't know I knew about the affair, about how, while he was in the shower one night after working a second shift, the phone rang sometime after midnight. I answered. It was his mistress, calling things off—she thought I was my mother. She told me to tell him it was over and to stop calling her. I think I apologized for him calling her, though I suppose, in retrospect, she was hoping to get things moving—to prompt my married father to leave his wife for her. I remember not being angry about the affair, just angry that he was off having a better life with someone else while I tended his children who needed so much more than I could ever give them. So when he said it was hard to stay, my heart jumped—the tiniest jump, hoping he would leave and take us all with him. I thought there could still be a chance at a normal life because it was my mother who insisted on God and no school and no real life to speak of. But when we pulled into the driveway and my mother walked out the door toward the car, angry that we'd been gone so long, he quickly fell into his way of pacifying her. As he flirted and made light of our delay, I knew not to let myself hope that my father's unhappiness would lead to anything of use for us kids.

End of Prayer

The spring after I turn sixteen I light incense in the living room. I watch it smolder in my mother's prayer corner, hoping its odor will hide my secret cigarette. My father isn't home, children are all tucked in, mother too, or so I think. I am cold and exhausted, overwhelmed by the scent of dish soap on my chapped hands. I lock the door, let the bathtub fill with hot water, light a candle and set it on the toilet next to a single stolen cigarette. I let my clothes drop, stare at my face in the mirror for a moment, thankful to look more like my father than my mother, or so I tell myself. Then I get to regretting his nose, my nose. I sit down in the tub, wincing against the heat. My skin turns pink and I reach for the cigarette and candle, light the smoke from the small flame on the blackened wick. Lean back, breathe in.

I think I could sleep beneath this hot water, my head relaxed against the smooth plastic, cigarette between the fingertips of my outstretched arm—ash in the toilet. My eyes close. The steam rises. Quiet. Then the banging begins, my mother's voice through the thin door, her fists smacking against the divide between our bodies.

"Rachel! Are you smoking in there?"

"No," I say, taking another long, beautiful drag.

"Don't lie to me! I can smell it. I should have known . . . you never light the incense."

She's right. I never light her blessed incense unless commanded, standing in the prayer corner watching my little brothers kiss their icons, my mother in her pink chair, ready to lead the prayers, the chants, her chubby fingers handling her prayer beads softly. Tonight, my fingers bring the cigarette to my lips for a final drag and then let the butt drop into the toilet. I resent the sound when water meets flame—the end of my last smoke.

"Answer me," my mother demands.

I finally call out that I'm washing my hair and then let my body slip down beneath the water. I hear her voice, distorted and angry, the doorknob shaking against the lock.

I dry off and dress before opening the bathroom door; my hair is more than damp and leaves wet spots on my shoulders and down most of my back. My mother rushes in, searching for the cigarette butt I flushed down the toilet. She follows me to the living room, gets close, her hands full with my hair. She brings it to her face and inhales. I know the scent of smoke is gone and let my eyes settle on her disappointed ones.

"Have you packed for the trip to Franklin tomorrow?" she asks, dropping my hair with disdain.

"No," I say.

"Don't forget a head covering."

"Ok."

"Excuse me?"

"I mean, yes, ma'am."

It takes about five hours to get to Saint Ignatius Church. Everyone crams into the van. The children misbehave, bored. My parents yell and threaten spankings. I try to zone out, lean against the window, at first watching the rolling hills, the thickening trees alongside the road, before shutting my eyes and daydreaming of the ballet studio I've not seen in nearly a year. I don't wonder why we can't go to the church closer to my house. I know it's because my mother has found something not to like about it. I know she has searched until she found a priest she likes well enough, one that, no doubt, humors her and holds his tongue about her not sending her children to school or seeking a job of her own, instead looking for charity while the kitchen cabinets remain stark.

My mother has been looking for the "right" faith for years—going through churches and never finding contentment in any of them for long. Now it is the Eastern Orthodox Church, and for a while she has been ready to make her conversion complete. My father goes along with the conversion, as does Ben, and of course, my little brothers and sister are not given a choice. Seth has not lived at home for a few years and has no interest in converting. I refuse conversion and, at sixteen, no one can make me stand before a priest. Here is one thing I cannot be forced to do and I am thankful.

I sit with the babies who color or play with Legos while I read. All of us kids are cooped in a spare bedroom at the priest's house because my mother has explained how there isn't money for a hotel. So the priest and his wife open up their home, but I know we are all a burden, I see it in the priest's wife as she eyes the boys, unkempt from travel and ready to stretch their legs. I look from her to the spotless living room, the beautiful tables and lamps, the things that would lose their luster in a matter of days in our house. So I take the babies and hide out of the way. But I'm constantly alert, waiting for the next break in calm. Sometimes the break comes with noise, a harsh yell, a mean word or a command spoken with a tone that is meant to wear me down. And I have come close to breaking, sometimes so tired that, if it were not for the smallness of my little sister's fingers clasped around my pinky as she sleeps, I might have slipped away. The easily opened window, the not-so-short jump from roof to ground, a highway seven miles away where I could hitch a ride to some other place. I've packed a bag many times, avoiding the sleeping child in my bed until it's time to kiss her goodbye. I've knelt down next to the bed, brushed her brown curls from her face, leaned in, and kissed her flushed cheek, and every time it's as if she knew I meant to leave her. She reached for my pinky, wrapped her fist around it, gave a sleepy coo, squeezed my finger tight, and it's always in that moment that I know I can't leave. And each time I pack, I get this notion that I won't look, won't say goodbye this time. And still, I give in to my sister's soft whimpers, her perfect face, her hold on my hand that reaches to that place in my chest where love beats too fierce to give permission for an escape.

But for now, in Franklin, escape isn't possible. My mother comes in the room with a large bowl of water in her hands. She insists the children leave, which makes me nervous. I worry about what they will do unwatched, so I stand to follow them, but she tells me to sit back down. There is a soft smile on her face and she is using her most gentle voice. My nervousness gives way to outright anxiety.

As a child I used to listen for any sound escaping my mother's throat, hoping to determine her mood by the pitch of her voice when she spoke. At one point, I thought I could tell what kind of mood she was in by the sound of her clearing her throat. If it was a light clearing sound, she would love me that day, maybe run her fingertips through my hair or feed me something wonderful. If it was lower, a deep clearing, she was unhappy, though I wouldn't know why; only that everything I did was the wrong thing and nothing would make it right. Older now, I understand that the clearing of her throat means nothing. Today, it's my mother's sweetest voice that escapes her lips, only instead of demanding something she seemingly wants nothing, which adds to my anxiety the way not knowing always does. She takes my book from my hands and closes it gently before setting it aside. Then she gets down on her knees, removes my shoes and socks, and begins to wash my feet and I notice the bowl seems to have some kind of scented oil in it that fights against the warm water, large yellow circles on a clear surface. I don't need to be told what scene my mother has playing in her mind, and yet I, hiding my horror, try to convince myself she isn't actually trying to offer a strange interpretation of Christ and the whore. I fight the urge to jerk away from her touch, to run from the room, an urge that becomes stronger when my mother says her hair is not long enough, is not like the real Mary Magdalene's. I fixate on the top of her head, her hair, dry, gray streaks intertwined with the darkness. A decade ago she kept her hair dyed blond and curled it with hot rollers. Her fingernails had been long and she painted them deep red, her skin, soft and smooth. As a child, I thought my mother the most beautiful woman in the world; as a teenager, I struggle to not wonder at the thickness of her body and the unhappy creases around her mouth.

"Tomorrow I'll officially become Magdalena," she says, looking up at me from her knees, "but today I wash you as Mary Magdalene washed the feet of Christ. I know the conversion is my choice. I understand you are not sure if you're ready, but what a beautiful thing, to join the church as a family, all of us together entering the one true faith for eternity."

"I'll think about it," I say, and put my socks and shoes back on, trying not to think of the pointe shoes I'd rather be putting on, trying not to notice my mother staring at me. I know her act of humility is insincere, an attempt to make me to do something I've already refused. She lies back on the thick carpet, moaning about the long drive and her not feeling well. I take her cue and clean up the mess, picking up the bowl and taking it to the bathroom where I pour the water down the sink. In the mirror I look at the skin around my neck, jaw, cheeks, and then finally my eyes. I feel sick and kneel down in front of the toilet.

I watch the children from the back of the church, the baptisms and chrismations completed in dark lighting and beneath a haze of smoking incense. Luke's dark brown eyes squint in anger against the crossing of the priest and at the tub of water he's to be immersed in. Noah tries to be brave as the priest gives him the Eucharist, tries not to cry when the wine-soaked bread touches his lips and tongue—his face quivers and finally, he gags. I want to grab him, want to grab all of them and flee.

Months later, I will get the chance to grab Luke up, though I won't get to flee. I will watch from the back of the church as the boys follow my father up to the priest for the Eucharist. Noah will again gag but be as brave as he possibly can, though his eyes will show his fear and it will hurt my heart to watch. Then Luke will refuse the blood and flesh of Christ by screaming at the priest "I won't do it, you big butthead!" I'm a little proud of him when he does this, I will certainly smile and hold down a laugh fast forming in my throat. But then, I will see the anger in my father's eyes and feel nervous for Luke, who will have turned on his heel, having leapt out of my father's reach, and will run for safety. He will run to me. And though he's a bit old for it, I will grab him up, will hold onto him tightly, even as my father will come to stand next to me, glaring, wanting to jerk Luke from my arms but knowing better than to do it in public. Today, in Franklin, my mother's smile is spread thin across her lips, my father looks at his feet or at the top of the boys' heads and for a minute, I am overcome with embarrassment by his awkwardness.

After my mother's official conversion to the Orthodox Church, I think perhaps things will change. And they do somewhat, because after nearly a year and much begging, I am allowed to take a ballet class again. What I don't tell my parents was that it is an audition class. In the year following my attempted overdose I'd given myself barre every night, preparing for the audition. After

I earn a spot in the company of high school girls, it occurs to me that I haven't thought much past the audition. I stare at the contract where it says, "parent or guardian sign here" for some time. Eventually, I breathe deep and try to calm my shaking hands as I place the contract inside one of my mother's spiritual books along with a flower I hand to her and beg one last time.

Later, after my parents discuss what I've done, they call me to the kitchen:

"Your mother has been speaking with church members about you and they have offered to fly you out to a monastery in Santa Rosa. We want you to go," my father says.

I am already shaking my head no before he finishes the sentence, remembering my refusal to convert with the family, loving that refusal.

"Look, if you go I'm more likely to sign your contract. If you don't go, I won't sign it at all."

I collapse in a chair by the kitchen table, look at the contract in my father's hands. It is unfolded and I can see the stain of my messy signature in blue.

"How long?" I finally ask.

"At least a few weeks, maybe longer."

Surprised my father is doing the talking, I look at my mother. Her face is grim, her lips twitching.

"I'll think about it," I say, wondering who would look after the babies in my absence. Eventually I agree to go to the monastery.

In Santa Rosa, California, nuns are nice, have promised to take me into the city for ballet classes, will help me earn my high school diploma. I can stay in the monastery all year round, though I would have to convert. The nuns, especially the Abbess, Mother Michaela, tell me to pray. So I pray, forehead one with the wooden floor. I pray between moments of sleep during what is meant to be an all-night vigil inside a small chapel tucked delicately among redwoods. The chapel isn't far from a rock quarry, a broken neighboring mountain, pulled apart, split open, and raided. The chapel is thick with incense and body odor seeping from beneath thick garments of nuns and the thin, long cotton skirts and shirtsleeves of girls. Prostrating is allowed, which is how I've come to the ground, shins flat against the floor, head bowed under the heat of it all. I think I might cry but I'm not sure, feeling no tears, sweat maybe, salty on my lips. Candles flicker against the soft yellow walls, casting a shaky glow against the sheen of freshly stained trim, and Byzantine icons look intensely at nothing. I'm supposed to pray for guidance, supposed to prepare myself for chrismation, supposed to choose a saint. I am supposed to pray. Mother Michaela tells me it's important and that conversion must not be done lightly.

I read books about saints, choose a saint because I like her name, Vasilissa, and because she was not a child bearer, because she gathered her fallen brethren and buried their flesh, the flesh that Nero had demanded lay out in the open to rot. I choose her because she was brave, because she died in defiance, because she was not the saint my mother chose for me, not Saint Rachel, beloved of Jacob, wife and mother.

At night I and the other girls who have been sent to the monastery stay in a dilapidated building halfway down the mountain. The building smells of must, is laid with orange shag carpet, and filled with bunk beds. Instead of going to bed, I slip out of the dorm, to the dirt road, and then off it and into the trees. I walk more than a few yards in search of Robyn. She's about twenty, four years older than me, and keeps a pitched tent near the road's edge. She sleeps, I think, in the same layers of thin cotton she wears every day, and each morning at vespers I notice her clothes wear a distinctly disheveled look. I find her tent and try to hope that she won't mind my visit. She doesn't seem to, and I think she is either perpetually kind and patient, ready to offer what she can to any person that might have some sort of need, or she actually wants company. Either way, I'm satisfied to be tolerated (or wanted) and ask her about the quarry, if she's been to the top, to the edge? She has, and leads me through the trees, kicking up dust, her boots pressing against fallen twigs that snap, sharp and quick beneath her weight.

"Be careful," she says, as we come to a clearing. "The edge is just there." She points a few feet ahead and my knees go weak, sink down to the ground, crouching like an animal, digits clawing at the earth for something to grab onto. My stomach has dropped at the sight of the quarry, dusty and light gray, reaching deep into the earth.

Robyn tells me she has hitchhiked to California in search of something, of God's forgiveness maybe. She found the monastery and decided to face her guilt straight on. She couldn't help her desire for women, she says, but she could try to tame it. She tells me it's wrong, that it's a sin, her desire. She doesn't want to be a sinner. We toss rocks into the quarry, and I wish it were a massive pool of water instead of an empty hole surrounded by all this rock and dirt. Later, I'll regret nodding calmly as I listened to her words, her attempt to set herself aright. I ought to have insisted her desire couldn't be wrong, that it didn't make her a sinner, that there was nothing to set right because she was already perfect. And she was, too. Robyn, tall and solid, who stepped with me to the outside of church when the priest told those who had not yet been baptized to remove themselves from the premises. She said she wanted to see, was curious about what was kept from us. I had no such curiosity, and I wondered if there was something wrong with me, that I couldn't feel more curiosity for God.

In the morning I walk down to the bottom of the hill for vespers. *It can't be so bad, living here*, I think. Why not stay, convert, be taken into town for ballet classes as Mother Michaela promises? *Why shouldn't you stay?* I push down the thought of the babies. I put them out of my mind because it's too hard—picturing their faces or the sound of their voices, their giggles, their everything. Instead I think about the smell of a marley floor, the feel of the barre in my hand, the music filling a studio. Push down thoughts of the babies. Push down the unease I feel at my diminishing belief in God.

When I call my parents to say I want to stay at the monastery, they lose it, especially my mother, who ignores Mother Michaela's pleas to let me stay and demands I be sent home. When I return home, my mother wastes no time in bad-mouthing the monastery.

"The monastery was evil; I knew it the second you said you wanted to stay," my mother says, "Thank God we got you back when we did. They wanted to turn you from us, from God."

I say nothing. Stare at my mother. Just stare.

"Why have you chosen another saint? I gave you the icon of St. Rachel because God told me it was for you. I chose all the saints for my children."

I calmly say I like Vasilissa better.

"You aren't in a monastery any longer! What is all this quiet whispering! Stop it!" my mother yells.

I don't want to yell back, but I know that's what she wants from me, and so I'm paralyzed, not out of fear but of not knowing what to do. I'd feel more anxious about not knowing if it were not for the heaviness pushing down upon my chest. There are the babies, looking at me, distrusting now because I had wanted to leave. It hurts, that distrust. It hurts because I know it's earned. I had pushed them down, the feeling of them, their need for me. So before sleep, I will once again make my plea for my mother's contentment, and with that plea I will find tears. I will beg. And then I will stop. And just as those beautiful babies come to trust me again, feel safe that I won't leave them, I will. I will leave shortly after I turn seventeen and I will not pray for forgiveness.

End of Tennessee

Tennessee land can seem to roll like waves too gentle to break, but it does break in some places. Limestone cuts cliffs alongside the Holston riverbank where my brothers and I used to sneak off to when we lived in Kingsport. We would go to jump in the river, and sometimes other kids would be there jumping too. It was mostly all boys who swam alongside my brothers, joining them in their chant of my name as I looked over the edge with hesitation. Eventually, I always jumped. And these random boys would say I was tough, but flat as hell, not knowing I could hear their whispers despite the cicadas' calls. I was maybe eleven and would blush dark red and pretend I hadn't heard.

It's April now; I'm a few months into seventeen and the hills are green, the dogwoods that line arching driveways are blossoming pink and white, and I sit next to my oldest brother who I do not trust, who has done things to me I force myself to forget, and I'll keep forcing myself until I cannot. I force myself even now, sitting in his car, smoking his cigarettes, and feeling welts swell bigger on my arms as I notice the beginning of bruises taking shape. At first I'd not felt the pain, but the sound of wood hitting flesh, the door slamming against my body, brought me to. Not even an hour earlier and I had been sitting at the end of my parents' driveway, waiting. I'd called my brother that morning, but he had been in Bristol getting high and he hadn't wanted to get involved. I called my sister-in-law, Darla, who made him get involved. It's somewhere around three o'clock now.

Earlier this morning I had a purse slung around my shoulder, and tucked inside was my birth certificate and social security card. I knew I needed these documents and that they would be hard to replace. I'd hidden another bag in the shed next to the house, planning to grab it the second my brother pulled into the driveway. But my mother suspected I was planning something and had watched me stash my bag from the window, and she had taken it while I was in the shower. The purse I had kept with me and slung over my head and across my chest as I headed out to the end of the driveway. I waited for my brother to show up. I waited for hours and recalled a past when I had loved my mother.

There she was, my mother, on a Saturday afternoon when I was five, fixing my hair in ribbons—long ones—pink, white, and blue. She sent me off to another child's birthday party. We lived on "The Property" then and I walked past the rows of apartment doors, feeling more and more guilty with every step. My brothers had gone to friends' houses to play and I watched my mother sigh sadly as they put their shoes on and made ready to leave. Later, as I begin walking down the hillside, I can't stop thinking of my mother all alone in the apartment again. Within minutes I turn back, ribbons whipping behind me. I wanted to go to the party, but my mother had nowhere to go, so I tell her to come to the party, too. She smiles, says it's not for adults, then hugs me and tells me I'm her sweet girl for coming back to her mother. Then the phone rings and my mother answers quickly. I sit on the floor staring up at her until she gets up from the couch and walks into the bedroom, shutting the door behind her. The thought of birthday cake enters my mind and I wonder about other treats that might have been at the party. Hungrily, I walk to the kitchen. I spread miracle whip on white bread, squish it into a ball, and then eat it like a roll.

It had been a few hours of waiting by the road, around lunchtime, when my mother sent the children out to the driveway with instructions that I get them ready for lunch. I ignored the instructions and urged them to go back inside. My little sister would not budge, so I picked her baby body up and walked her inside. I wasn't all the way through the doorway before my mother flew at me, fists flying, landing erratically as I shielded my little sister and slowly let her slide to the floor. That's when my mother saw the purse and grabbed it, but I caught the strap and held on. She went to her bedroom, I followed, still holding onto the purse. She was quick, turned before I had my body through that doorway, just my arm and my right foot. That's when the slamming began. And the sound and the pain and the insanity of it all made me let go. My mother ran to the bed, lay on it rocking back and forth and hugging the purse with one arm, crossing herself over and over with the other saying, "Lord Jesus Christ, Son of God, have mercy on me!" I started to work the straps out of her fingertips, but quickly I gave up. The babies were all crying, all watching me, watching her be crazy, watching me not be the me they knew. I walked back out to the driveway and waited while my baby sister beat her fists against the window.

I was not sure how much time passed after I left my mother there rolling in her bed, more than half an hour, less than a full one. I leaned against the neighbor's fence post, the final one dividing his pristine yard from our dumpy one, and I stared at the woods, the wide ditch at the base of the hill, and the spring weeds already as tall as my knees. Logan came out carrying my sister. Noah, Luke, and Michael followed. They put themselves in the car and I did my best not to let them see me looking. Then my mother walked out, completely recovered from her fit. I hate when my mother is alone in the car with the kids, but I kept telling myself to stay put. And when my mother walked past the van and neared where I sat, I did not move. When she tossed my purse at my feet I felt a small amount of relief in my chest and I let myself reach for it. And just as I did so, she said, "But here's what you really wanted," and sprinkled bits of my birth certificate, social security card, and the numbers for help on the ground in front of me.

She waited, knowing I'd want to scoop up the papers but wouldn't, not in front of her. Finally, she said, "Get in the car, we are going to McDonald's."

I ignored her and did not move. When I heard her steps shuffle gravel and the van door slammed shut, I still do not move. When she pulled out of the driveway and out of sight, I picked up the pieces knowing the damage was irreversible.

The air was heavy with humidity and my hair stuck to my neck and face. My mother returned, walked toward me and still I did not move.

"I brought you some lunch," she said in her sweetest, most gentle voice.

I ignored her, stared into the ditch, wished like hell my brother would show up. My mother cooed, "Rachel, you have to eat."

She took a step further and I looked at her face; she was trying to appear tender. I stared straight into her eyes and fear moved throughout my body as I realized a ride might never come. Then I calmed myself, knowing I could hitchhike if I really had to.

"I don't want it," I said to my mother.

Her face tightened then took on a look that was something like anger, something like mockery. She dropped the food on the ground in front of me and went inside. I sat with the food at my feet for a few minutes and then my brother finally arrived. I immediately jumped into the car.

"What the fuck is happening?" he asked.

"Just please let's go," I'd said, buckling my seatbelt and looking over my shoulder, worried that someone, anyone, might show up and try to stop me.

"God damn it. I can't leave without saying anything," he'd said in a tone that scared me into worry—afraid he wouldn't take me out of Rogersville after all. Instinctively, I locked the car doors.

He went inside and some five minutes passed before he

came back out carrying the bag my mother had taken from me. He threw it in the back seat and then got behind the wheel. He backed the car out in a fury.

"God, she's a fucking crazy bitch," he says.

He lights a cigarette, then hands me the pack. I light one too and then hand Seth the bag of food my mother had thrown on the ground.

"She thought I'd stay if she gave me a cheeseburger."

"Right, because she's always been so good about feeding her kids."

I nod, look ahead, and see the highway nearing. We stop at the one-way stop before pulling out onto Highway 70. On the right Brightshore Market seems still, though I know live bait is making circles in their tanks and worms nestle thick into dark, wet soil.

My brother opens the bag of food, takes a bite, and slowly chews.

"Might as well not let it go to waste," he says.

He drives onto the highway and I lean forward, palms against the dash, tense until we get out of Rogersville and to Churchill, Seth's town. Then I can breathe for a minute and plan my next move. I take another drag, the nicotine making me the tiniest bit dizzy, and Tennessee just rolls on.

Darla, my sister-in-law, twenty-one, skinny with huge blue eyes and dark curls, hugs me in the front yard of her and my brother's house. Her mother, who lives next door, waves from the window. A cigarette trembles between Darla's long fingers. She inspects my body and tears up.

"What are we going to do?"

"I'm going to Indiana," I say. "My old ballet teacher is there now—she'll help."

A look of both worry and relief comes over Darla's face.

"I want you to stay," she says.

"You know my parents will do everything they can to hurt you."

"We can get a lawyer," she says.

"We don't have that kind of money."

"I'm making your favorite cheesy potatoes for dinner," Darla offers hopefully as she lights another cigarette and sighs.

The next day my brother drives me a few miles down the road to a gas station alongside the highway. Sophia, the one friend I had made at the ballet, is waiting in her car, her boyfriend at the wheel looking awkward in his tie and gelled hair. Sophia looks beautiful though, all dressed up for a school dance, her hair high on her head, her lips painted pink. She gives me the sixty dollars I'd called and asked for the night before, which I promised to pay back. She hugs me and asks if we can take one last picture together. I nod, and she motions for her boyfriend to get out of the car. He turns on the camera, and my brother, who has been leaning against his car, high and bored, gets in and closes the door behind him. I know it's time to leave, so I wrap one arm around Sophia's waist and pull the other behind my back to hide the bruises from the lens. Sophia's dress is a deep red, my shirt a bright red. Her one arm is around my waist, the other delicate at her side, her wrist pale and lovely, wrapped in a corsage of white roses and baby's breath.

I plan to meet the receptionist, Mindy, from the ballet in Kingsport the next day. We were to meet at the public library and from there she was going to take me to the bus station. When I spoke to her on the phone she said she knew this day would come, though she said she was surprised it hadn't come sooner. Having a plan to leave Tennessee gives me a little peace and in the evening I sit with Darla in her living room watching television and eating ice cream. I feel sad about the fact that I might not ever see her again after tonight, but as I'd done with the babies, I shut down those feelings as best I can—I cannot let that hurt get in the way of my escape. I take one of her cigarettes from the living room coffee table and walk out to the back porch, take a drag, and close my eyes. I try to hear the kind of music that filled ballet studios and theatres, to believe I could have freedom, to convince myself I'll find a way to save the babies. Some people might have called that hope, but it was just a story I told myself to believe. And I will believe, for years, until it is all too late. But right now, I smoke, I breathe, and then I hear the sound of tires crunching worn down asphalt, a car engine running in the driveway, and my sister-in-law slamming the back door as she dashes out of the house and grabs my arm.

"It's your mom! I'm hiding you in the basement."

"Okay," I say and follow her down the back stairs.

She hides me behind boxes of Christmas decorations and baby clothes my niece had outgrown.

"Don't worry, my mom will be here in a minute," Darla says, and runs back upstairs.

I hear my mother's voice—full of indignation and lacking control. Then I hear Darla and her mother's voices, telling my mother to go home because there isn't anything here for her. I can tell my mother tries to go in the house, but Darla's mother blocks the door.

"Lady, go home."

My mother declares she will be back and with the cops. But she doesn't return. It's my father who shows up the next morning. This time I walk out to meet him. Seth and Darla sit in the living room. Darla is nervous and worried and Seth is impatient. I tell them I'm not letting them get in trouble for me and then walk out the door.

My father's eyes are dark, darker than usual, the way they get when he's especially angry. He approaches me and I keep my ground, stare back at his angry eyes with equal rage.

"You can have your little vacation," he begins, "but if you aren't on my doorstep first thing Monday morning I'll have a warrant out for your arrest and I'll file a complaint against Seth and Darla for harboring you."

"Look at me," I say. "I'm never going back to that house."

"Like I said, be on my doorstep Monday morning or I'll call the cops."

"Call them," I say, stretching out my limbs covered in marks my mother left.

I utter these words with confidence, but the truth is I don't know if the cops will care. I hear that cases involving teenagers come down to their word against the parents', and it's usually the parents' word that carries the most weight. It does the trick though, and I see worry flash across my father's face. But then he composes himself.

"You don't look that bad. Besides, I saw what you did to your mother," he replied.

"I didn't do anything to her."

"That's not what she or the injuries on her body say."

"You know I didn't do anything to her."

He doesn't argue with me then. Even he knows my mother's lie that I hurt her would not hold, not with all the medical records out there bearing witness to my mother's tendency to self-inflict wounds and the fact that I'd never raise a hand to her. Though with less confidence, he says again, "Monday morning or I'll press charges against Seth and Darla, and I'll have you arrested as a runaway."

I stand there and watched him walk away. Darla steps out and stands next to me, lights two cigarettes and hands me one.

"What are we going to do?" she says, releasing a cloud of smoke into the air.

"I'm getting the fuck out of Tennessee," I say.

The next morning, I sit in the foyer of the Kingsport Public Library. The book smell is in the air, the tiled floor cracked and dirty. A public phone booth is built into the east wall. I walk over and sit on the swiveling stool in front of the phone, notice the pad and pen lying next to a phone book, take them up and write a note to my father. A librarian walks out the library doors, through the lobby, and outside with cigarettes in her hand. I quickly shove the note in my purse and return to the bench to sit next to my bag. The librarian comes back in, coughs, then asks, "School out today?"

Just then Mindy walks in, saving me from stuttering out a lie. She nods to the librarian and takes my bags.

"Are you ready?" Mindy asks.

"Yes," I say and gather up my things.

Mindy drives me to the bus station and gives me cash to buy a bus ticket.

"I'm glad you're finally leaving. It's the right thing. But remember, you can't tell anyone I helped you. I could get in a lot of trouble," she says.

"I know. I promise I won't say a word. And I'll pay you back as soon as I can."

"You don't worry about that. I just wish I could give you more."

"You better go," I say, feeling anxious.

"I'll leave once the bus pulls away," she says, with a half-smile.

The man in the seat behind mine pushes down the top of a brown bag to show me its contents—Southern Comfort—and offers me a sip, which I do not take. He asks what happened to me.

"Nothing," I say and pull my sleeves down below my wrists, remembering how my father hated my habit of doing so, how he said it made me look sloppy.

Every time I start to doze off, I see Luke running toward me, a giggle in his throat, his dark eyes lit up, waiting for me to squish him like I did every day. I wake up quickly to the feeling of weight upon my chest and sickness in my stomach, and the sound of the Greyhound humming slowly along the highway. I do my best not to close my eyes, to distract myself from the babies.

I get off the bus and hitchhike to the Fort Wayne Ballet, the school and company my teacher from Tennessee has taken over. I remember when she left Tennessee and she hugged me, held my face in her thin hands and said, "Of all my students you are the one I most don't want to leave behind. If I could, I would take you with me."

My throat hurt and eyes threatened to wet, but I did not let myself cry. I'd just nodded and bit my cheeks. She had told me if it ever became too much that I could always come to her. Looking back, I'm not sure how I ever believed this was a good idea, but I suppose that's what feeling desperate does to a person.

When I show up at the ballet I find my teacher in her office. When she sees me she stands up quickly, a confused look on her face. Then it hits me I've done the wrong thing, gone to the wrong place. For whatever it's worth, I know she wanted to mean those words, but the truth was the trouble was just too much—too many legal implications and she had her own family to worry about.

I think I should have looked for my cousin who had been my favorite when I was little and still living in Texas. I heard he was living in Oklahoma—I should have found him and gone there instead.

"I just need a little time to work and save some money," I

say, wondering if my mother will also think to find my cousin, to tell him not to help me.

My teacher seems finally to realize what I've done. She moves from behind her desk toward me, pulls me close in a hug, then takes my hand and leads me to the vacant office next to hers.

"Don't move. Don't turn the lights on. Just wait here. I'll be right back," she says.

She walks away and I stand still, afraid to move, wondering if maybe I should just bolt out of the ballet altogether. I hear my teacher talking down the hallway. Another woman's voice interrupts hers. She sounds irritated.

"If the situation is as bad as you say it is, of course she would leave when told her you would help. Jesus Christ, Jenna."

"I don't know. I just wanted her to know she wasn't alone. I don't know . . ."

"Where is she?" the other woman asks.

I hear both women walking toward the office where I'm standing in the darkness. My teacher introduces me to Elena, the ballet's marketing director. Elena looks me over and I feel my face get pink when I look down at my disheveled overalls, my sweatshirt tied around my waist, and I notice for the first time how faded my favorite tank top has become.

"Well, you can't send her back," Elena says.

My teacher nods, worried.

"Do you want to stay with me for now until we sort some things out?" Elena asks.

I nod because I don't know what else to do. My ballet teacher asks me if I need anything.

"Toothpaste," I say.

She gives me twenty dollars. Months later, when it's safe, she gives me clothes to wear in ballet class and works it out so I don't have to pay for classes. But right now she stands in the doorway looking unsure, something I've never seen in her before.

Elena orders food at a drive-thru and asks what I want. I tell her I'm not hungry. She orders something anyway. On the drive to her apartment, she points out that my teacher is going through a divorce, a custody battle, and harboring a runaway could cause her some real problems.

"It'll be nicer at my apartment anyway. It will be quiet, and you'll have a chance to rest," Elena says.

Her apartment is the entire first floor of an old house in a historic neighborhood. She shows me the bed in her spare room, where she keeps the television remote, and the fresh towels in the linen closet. She picks up her keys and I follow her to the back door.

"The food is in the fridge," she says and goes back to work.

I notice how nice her house is—the hardwood floors, tall ceilings, and the smell of lemons. I'm afraid to touch anything, but finally give into tiredness and crawl into the bed in the spare room. From the early noon hour well into the night's darkness, I sleep.

I wake up with a jolt, and then hear Elena talking on the porch, saying she didn't know what else to do. She's talking into a phone. I feel shame for being a nuisance. I get up and make the bed, go to the bathroom. Then return to the spare room and sit at the foot of the bed, unsure of what to do. The screen door creaks when Elena opens it, shutting it softly behind her.

She calls out, "Are you awake?"

"Yes," I say and walk into the living room.

"Let's go to dinner," Elena says energetically.

I tell her I don't have money for that and she says it's her treat. We go to an Italian restaurant, and I look at the prices and feel worried about ordering. I look for something cheap and order that.

Elena is gregarious, a beautiful redhead with enormous green eyes that are hard not to stare at. I've never seen eyes like that and tell her so. She smiles and tells me she gets that a lot. She doesn't ask me about my family, just what kind of food I like, what my favorite subject is, and other things like that—things no one has ever really asked me before. I tell her I don't like garlic and she gasps.

"What do you mean you don't like garlic? It's an essential food group!" she declares.

"I just don't, I guess."

"Oh my god. I'm Italian. Garlic is a way of life."

"Oh. Well, maybe I can try it again. I guess I've only ever had it in pill form."

"Well, yeah, that's disgusting. Of course you don't like those. I'll make fish with garlic sauce this weekend. You may like it," Elena says.

"Okay," I say, nervous about everything.

I call my sister-in-law from a pay phone to see if she knows how my brothers and sister are doing. She tells me that my mother put out a warrant for my arrest. So for weeks I do nothing but hide out at Elena's and in the library, unsure of what do with myself. Elena cooks food that's so good it seems to melt in my mouth. I didn't know food could be like that. She takes me for a haircut, takes me to the movies, takes me around to meet her family. She worries I'm going insane with boredom. And she's right, but more than anything I feel guilt. Pressure. I need to make something happen so that someday I could make something happen for my siblings. And I need to not be anyone's burden. Though Elena will never say it, I know it's crazy and difficult to have a random teenager in her house. I feel the pressure of my interference into her life constantly. It isn't until I move to another state that Elena will remind me of what I owe her, though she will do so subtly. Right now, though, I think, *Fuck it*, apply for a job at a fast-food restaurant by the library because depending on the kindness of strangers, of hiding out at their expense, fills me with shame. So I get a job and think that maybe my parents never did put out a warrant, but when I show up for my first day of work a detective is there waiting for me.

"You have to come with me," he says.

We don't go far, just a short walk across a small parking lot to his car. We wait for a patrol car to come pick me up. I'm quiet for a bit, then blurt out, "The woman I was staying with didn't know I was a runaway."

I'm taken to a juvenile detention center. On the drive over the officer asks me why I ran away. I say nothing and shrug my shoulders, my face burning. I don't know how to talk about life with my parents, and there are some things I don't want known.

And even if I could find the words, my mother could always say I was a liar, and say it she would. I sit back—*eight more months and I'll be legal age*. The months felt like eternity.

I look through the partition, look for the eyes of the officer in the rearview mirror.

"Are you going to take my bag away?"

"I won't, but the people at the detention center will."

"Will my parents get it before me, do you know?"

"It's possible."

I'm quiet for a moment. I'd written all these notes and letters to my father starting that day in the Kingsport Public Library. They are letters I'd never send, but wrote nonetheless. Angry letters asking why he'd let things happen the way they did. The letters were long and messy, but they were specific. I couldn't bear the thought of my mother going through my letters, interpreting them for my father, never giving him the chance to read them himself. Or worse, he would see them and say nothing. Silence. He was so good at silence.

"Is there any way I can throw some stuff away? Just some papers I've written on?"

"There is a trashcan in front of the center."

I prepare the letters for the trashcan by tearing them into pieces. The officer watches me but says nothing. When we get out of the car, he points to the trashcan and I toss my writing in it, the papers now surrounded by wadded up fast food bags and soda cups with straws jutting out.

Inside the detention center I'm checked in by somewhat terse staff. I answer their questions briefly, quick and quiet.

I'm part angry, part depressed. That afternoon while sitting in a common room of plastic blue cushions, white cinder block walls, and girls my age, a lady comes in and takes me to her office. She is probably in her fifties and there are wrinkles around her eyes, which are bright behind thick glasses. She takes a deep breath, exhales in a tired way.

"I watched you throw this away from the window," she says, handing me a baggie full of torn pieces of paper.

I take the bag and stare at it as she continues.

"I started reading through those and stopped myself. I don't know what all has happened to you and I don't think I want to know. But you don't belong in here. Take those back. Keep them with you. You are entitled to see a lawyer. Did you know that?"

I shake my head no.

"Do you want to talk to the lawyer here?"

"I don't have any money," I say.

"You don't need money to talk to her. It's your right, if you want it."

"I want it."

The lawyer is also somewhere around fifty, thin, and has hair that reaches sharply down to her jaw line. She asks me why I ran away. I pick things to tell her that I think will matter the most, like not going to school. She says she'll talk with the woman who found my letters and was there anything else I wanted to tell her. I sit there for a minute, pondering, feeling shame, troubled in a way I cannot articulate.

"If you know what the letters say, do I have to say it right now, too?" I ask.

"No. But you need to be prepared for the possibility for some of it to come out in court."

I take a breath. "Okay."

At the courthouse I'm greeted by a caseworker or probation officer—I'm never quite clear who he is. He takes me to a room where my parents are waiting. My father asks him to take off my handcuffs, which leads to my mother placing a loving hand on my father's shoulder.

"Have a seat," the unknown man says.

I sit. Feeling heat in my face as I look at this man, confused as to who he is supposed to be to me.

"So you just up and left your siblings a few months ago?" he says.

"What?" I say.

"Your parents tell me you left home, left your little brothers and sisters. As your mother and I were talking about before you were here, you have to know if you aren't at home to tell your siblings you love them, they will think you don't."

"That's not true. They know I love them," I say.

"No they don't. Children forget things and if you aren't there to remind them they will forget. Already they think you don't care about them," the man states.

I am overcome with incredible rage when I look to my mother, who is almost smiling at me. She knows the way to look, to sound, to behave. That part of me that knows how to hate comes out and I turn to the unknown man and look directly in his eyes.

"Go to hell," I say.

My father reacts, forgetting the handcuffs, a dark stare, angry voice, "You don't talk like that, young lady!"

"Fuck you," I say.

My mother gasps, an actual smile appears on her face as I give her the reaction she's wanted all along.

"You see," my mother says calmly. "She's very rebellious."

I wonder about the help the lawyer said I would have, where she is, and I begin to see there is not hope. If I could, if it wouldn't really make me crazy, I'd scream. But I sit back down and say nothing.

"I can see we have nothing to talk about," the unknown man says, opens the door and tells someone to escort me out.

I'm taken to a bench in front of the courtroom next to a girl about my age.

"What are you here for?" she asks.

"I ran away from home. You?"

"Too much to get into," she replies with a laugh. "You want to go back home?"

"No."

"Well, you tell the judge and these people whatever they want to hear. Then you get out of here and just take off again. It's as easy as that," she says.

"You think so?"

"Yeah! I do it all the time. Just don't get caught like I do. Ya know, don't do anything stupid."

The girl is taken away by an officer and shortly after I'm taken to a courtroom, where I am told to sit at a table in front of the judge, who glances at me briefly through thick glasses. The unknown man sits at his own table on the right side of the judge, and my parents sit in chairs a few rows behind my table.

"So you ran away from home because you want to go to school?" the judge says more than asks.

"Yes, and other reasons, too," I say.

"And the state of Tennessee requires that you be registered with the school system."

"Yes, sir," I say.

My mother calls out from behind me, "She's lying! That's not true. She's lying!"

"Ma'am," the judge says, "that was a rhetorical question. Tennessee does require registration. Please remain in your seat quietly."

I did not turn around to look at my mother as she sat down, but I imagined she was defiant, staring at the judge. My father probably looked at him, too, or else stared not too particularly at anything. I'm surprised by my mother's outburst. She had been so calm earlier, had known how to speak to the unknown man, but now she sounds frazzled.

"The fact is there are some real problems here . . ." the judge is saying when my mother interrupts him.

"The only problem is Rachel! She's a liar and . . ." my mother is quickly interrupted by the judge.

"Ma'am, do not interrupt me. I won't tell you again. The next time you will be removed." He looks at me.

"As I was saying, there are some real problems here, but this is a matter for Tennessee, a case for their jurisdiction. Will you go back with your parents and have your case heard in Tennessee?"

"Yes, sir," I say, knowing I won't.

I do not trust Tennessee and I'll not return, so I lie to the judge, and when I turn around, my mother, pride wounded, will not look at me, but in the car she perks up, begins talking about life as if nothing strange was happening. I say nothing when she asks me a question. She turns around and looks at me from the front seat.

"You really think you could get away with any of this?"

I stare out the window.

"It's okay, you don't have to answer, it's a rhetorical question," she says sarcastically.

I notice my father is driving toward Elena's neighborhood and I realize that my parents have learned that I'd been staying with her. They pull in front of her house.

"I'll go in alone. It isn't right for us to be there without her knowing and she's probably at work," I say.

"Oh, she's not at work. She's in jail. That's right. Jail. See what your little stunt caused? She's just lucky I didn't press charges."

I get out of the van and both parents follow me closely.

"You know what," I say, "I don't want my stuff. We shouldn't go in her house when she's not there."

"Oh no. We're getting your stuff," my mother says as both parents come toward me. I raise my hand to throw the house key into some bushes across the street, but before I can release the key from my fist, my father lunges at me and so does my mother. Both of them dig at my closed fist, together prying at my fingers, trying to bend them open while my father pins my other arm down at my side. My hand is bleeding and so are both my father's by the time they manage to get the key. They let themselves in and my mother walks around the house inspecting things, my father looks around, too. He finds my bag.

"See," my mother says, "she's packed your things. She doesn't want you here anymore."

Elena's cat, who usually hid when new people were around, surprisingly, comes out despite all the commotion. I go to pet her goodbye. My mother, still inspecting the place, sees me bent down with the cat.

"Of course she has a cat," my mother says.

I kiss the cat's soft grey fur and then get up and walk past my mother, toward the kitchen, toward the back door. My father puts my bag down and starts walking toward me. I move quicker, go for the back door and feel my heart beating hard as my mother says his name in an alarmed tone. I know he is behind me and I move faster, get the door open, and, just as I'm nearly clear of the doorway, feel my father try to grab me. He gets a hold of the purse strap that I wear across my chest and down my back. I'm jerked back a little when he grabs the strap, but I recover quickly and lean all my weight forward, my hands at the doorframe, pulling with all my might. The strap snaps and sets me free. I run. I hear my father chasing after me, but I'm faster than him.

After a while I stop running. Catch my breath while looking all about me. Quickly I walk to St. Joseph's Hospital, thankful for the cool air that hits my face as the automatic doors slide open. I sit in a lobby chair for a while, watching people come and go, some stopping at the information desk, some carrying flowers, some looking exhausted and unkempt. *Seventeen*, I keep thinking, so close to eighteen. I feel tired as I walk to the pay phone and call Elena's office, afraid she won't answer, that my being in her house had banished her to jail for who knew how long. But she answers.

"They told me you were in jail," I blurt out.

"Well, I was at the police station. I wasn't in a cell or anything. It wasn't that bad. But Rachel, where are you? You can't run again. People who helped you can get into a lot a trouble."

"I know," I say.

When Elena picks me up, I tell her how my parents got into her house, that I'd tried to stop them, but now they have the key.

"Don't worry about that right now. Are you hurt?"

"No, I'm fine," I say.

We drive along in quiet for a bit, then Elena says, "The detective who arrested you is meeting us at the detention center to try and intervene with your parents. I called him to tell him I have you, that we are coming in, but that I'm not leaving you there all by yourself. He's been very candid. He's fed up with your parents—they've caused a lot of trouble. He says his counterpart in Tennessee feels pretty much the same."

"Really?"

"Yes, but don't get your hopes up. We still don't know what's going to happen. And listen, if worse comes to worst, if they make you go back with your parents, you can always come here again when you turn eighteen. There will be a place for you here."

I don't want anyone else in trouble because of me and can't figure out how it is that kind people could be punished while my parents got to go on being cruel. I just sit there and nod, say okay, but already I am planning to run again, maybe while driving back to Tennessee, maybe in Tennessee, but well before I get back to my parents' house. I know I would never be strong enough to leave the babies twice, and I probably wouldn't be strong enough to survive living in that house again.

At the detention center the detective sits next to me in the lobby.

"You know, after dealing with your parents over the last few days, I don't know how you lasted as long as you did. I'd have left years ago." This man's kindness makes me cry.

"You would have?" I manage to whisper.

"I would have," he says, pats my shoulder before continuing. "I told your father that you're just going to keep running. Why not let you go, let you stay here where you have people that care about you. I hope I've convinced him."

"Does my mother know?" I ask.

"We will find out," he says, looking out of the glass walls of the lobby as my parents pull up.

Elena is outside on her cell phone, and, not knowing what my parents look like, goes right on having her conversation. The detective tells me to stay put and quickly walks outside. He says a word to Elena and she quickly hangs up the phone. My mother must have figured out who she is because she goes straight toward her and throws my house key at her and then lunges at her. Elena takes a few steps back and remains calm as the detective steps in front of my mother who has begun to yell. After a few minutes my mother storms inside; I can see she has lost control, my father follows her in, his t-shirt stretched tight over a protruding belly. He glares at me, but I don't move. Workers at the facility have come to observe. The woman who had returned my letters steps in and tells my mother to calm herself. The detective stands between me and my father.

Elena comes and sits next to me, which sends my mother into further frenzy. She looks at me and says, "We don't want you back anymore," then looks at the detective and points at Elena, "but I don't want her staying with that woman!"

My father tells my mother to get in the car or he'll leave without her and storms out to the parking lot. As they drive away, I see my packed bag through the window. The detective says as long as I stay in his jurisdiction he can protect me from my parents. So I do. He thinks I should stay with someone besides Elena, just to avoid possible complications with my mother.

A local Orthodox priest, Father George, and his wife, Helen, a schoolteacher of children with special needs, are contacted. I end up staying in their unfinished basement until I turn eighteen. Out of respect, I go to church once a week, to vespers, while I stay with them, even though they know I don't believe. I feel relieved that I can begin working on my life, on school, on getting a job. Still, I always feel myself a burden on the people who had given me so much, like Elena, Father Michael and

Helen, strangers who chose to let me become close with them. I try not to dwell on all the debts I owe for all the kindness I received, but it's difficult. And when I'm nineteen I leave Indiana for the University of Utah's ballet program, housed in a place I've never seen, a place where I am excited to start fresh, to be a burden to no one. At first I feel forlorn, though soon enough that feeling subsides and I grow to love Utah—the mountains with many canyons full of redbud and aspen trees, the red desert in the south, and the air void of humidity. I've figured out that the West can get in your blood and the mountain air and desert dirt can settle in your bones. Slowly, I began to lick my wounds.

Dislocations

I met Jonah the first year I moved to Utah—I was nineteen, but we did not start dating until I was twenty-three. We live together for about ten months until I can no longer bear it. I wonder how he bore it. Our nights when we sometimes cook come with little conversation. The hot water falling a steamy white from the faucet, filling the cooking pot only halfway to the brim. I lift the pot from the sink onto the burner, turn the knob to spark the flame. My gaze shifts from the water to Jonah, who, at this moment is placing napkins on the small table in the corner of the kitchen. In the future when I think of Jonah, he will be my on-again, off-again boyfriend of much of my twenties. I loved his dark curls, tattoos, his forearms, and the way he pushed his shirt sleeves up to his elbows with carpenter hands revealing his lean muscles as he reclined in my living room with a book in his hands. And I hated his possessiveness, his desire for a version of me that did not exist. I will think of the times we had been cruel, unfaithful, unhappy. On this day, I watch Jonah eat the dinner I prepared, and when his face is quiet for a moment his blue eyes make their way to mine. Instantly I look away because I don't want to see him search my face for something more, something meaningful.

I try to hang pictures on my walls to keep them from looking stark and bright like the hallways of a hospital. I even hung a blanket that had a ballet dancer woven into the soft cotton. I hated it, took it down, and instead of returning it to my closet where it had been stored, delivered it to Goodwill. My mother sent that blanket to me a few years after I left home, the one time she actually had my address. In the blanket she had wrapped pictures of my younger siblings, awkwardly posed, dressed in clean clothes, but their hair was uncombed and their feet bare. I imagined those five little faces staring at the camera, their bodies longing to squirm away, annoyed by the forced posing, but curious about the attention our mother gave them in preparing them for their photos. I wondered if she had taken those just to send to me, to remind me of who I abandoned when I ran away from her. I don't need any reminding. Even my dreams are filled with the voices of my little brothers and sister—dreams that are interrupted by memories of the dark, wet mud of southern ground, the patches of drywall inside our farmhouse—dank humidity, a damp stench, a kind of prison from which escape is nearly impossible.

Jonah looks at me hard. I see it and feel it, his eyes struggling to focus. He reaches for me, breathing heavy, grips my body, knuckles slowly turning white, his mouth finding mine. This is the kind of thing that happens with Jonah—him pushing me to be affectionate, sexual, though I've explained how most of the times it makes me feel ill to be so. I've told him to find sex with another because I do not know how to give my body or to hold on to another's without it feeling all wrong. The edge of the bed gets smaller and smaller; I cannot get any closer to it without falling off. Jonah sleeps now, rolls over in his sleep moaning and reaching out to hold me. I press a little closer to the edge, but it's no use, his reach is far.

I get up, tiptoe quietly so as not to wake him. He doesn't stir and I slowly begin to let myself breathe, and then walk into the kitchen to make tea. I lift myself up on the countertop and sit there with the light off for a few moments, but it's too difficult to sit still, so I let my legs stretch toward the floor, look in the direction of the bedroom, then turn the back door handle and step outside with bare feet. My skin is cold and shows through the washed-up fabric of Jonah's white t-shirt, which looks silver in the moon's soft light. I reach for the pack of cigarettes from the empty planter box that rests in front of the kitchen window, light one, take a drag, exhale, and watch the smoke cloud rise and disappear. A moment of calm passes over me; it's the kind of calm I always feel right before remembering something I've tried so hard to forget—the warm, unwanted hand slowly moving up my leg, stops briefly, a short-lived hesitation. I dash the half-smoked cigarette against the brick wall of my apartment and step back inside. I take the tea to bed with me and watch a line of steam flow a few inches above the mug, holding it tightly to warm my palms and fingertips. I lean back onto the pillows and let my eyelids close. Jonah rises up on an elbow, leans over and places a kiss on my cheek, and then brushes my lips with his with the expectation of returned affection. I can't give it, my lips are stiff and cold, but he is satisfied with the warmth of my breath and lets his body sink back down beneath the covers.

The first big snow of the year has fallen on the Wasatch Range and with it comes a thick frost that coats the outer layer of my windows. It has come in the darkness, calm, like a soft blanket, beneath which lies time, frozen under the spell of winter. Back in Tennessee the winters had been quiet, except for the occasional dusting of snow, or a quick beating of frozen water, hail aiming for the ground with a vengeance, leaving black ice on back roads and highways. I'd driven on those slick roads, once. I was eighteen then, finally brave enough to go back to the house I'd run away from nearly two years earlier. The night had been especially dark and only a few cars were on the road. It was almost Christmas and I needed to see my brothers and sister.

Sleet fell in thick sheets, a ghostly veil against the black night. In the passenger seat of a borrowed car sat a package of cupcakes, chocolate with red and green icing. I felt lucky when I arrived at the farmhouse and discovered my parents were not home. The house was filthy and had no decorations, no signs of the holiday. The kids were watching television in the living room but tore themselves away from the screen long enough to follow me into the kitchen, shyly they looked from me to the package in my hand. I opened the box of cupcakes. Samantha and Michael each eagerly took one, but Logan, Noah, and Luke restrained themselves, their large eyes gazing at me, and not the cupcakes, as they slowly reached inside the box. The boys returned to their television show to eat their cake, but Samantha stayed next to me in the kitchen, near the counter where the remaining treats taunted her hungry eyes. She smiled at me and eyed the cupcakes. "Do you want another one?" I asked. She nodded and I handed her a cupcake. The icing added another layer of stickiness to the dirt that was already caked on her cheeks and hands. Her smile was nearly a grin, toothy and wide, her brown curls were messy, her bony body too small for a four-year old, and I wished more than anything that I could steal her away. I focused on her tangled hair, matted in places. I wetted a washcloth with warm water and used it to wash her face and hands, and then I put clean clothes on her little body, tossing the dirty dress she'd worn inside out in the laundry. She loved the attention, patient and still, even when I pulled at the tangles in her fine hair. She grinned while brushing her teeth, staring at her reflection in the mirror.

"Did I get it all?" she asked and then bared her teeth to me after a final pasty spit.

The waitress fills our mugs with bitter coffee and Jonah reaches for the tiny porcelain pot filled with creamer. His eyes are on me; I feel them before I even look up. I know the blue beneath his long eyelashes is roving over my face as I reach for the Tabasco and douse my food in it and stay on me when I add a bit of ketchup for sweetness. I finally return his blue stare. This time it is Jonah's gaze that drops as he tells me he needs something, someone who can show they care, just a little. I tell him about my great-grandfather, how he'd always burned his food before coating it in Tabasco.

"Did you hear me?" he asks in frustration.

"Yes, I heard," I say.

I hope he'll just let it go, but he doesn't. He pushes his plate away, reaches across the table and touches the top of my hand gently.

"I like your hands. I like when you touch me with them," he says.

I fight back the impulse to jerk my hand away from his, to make fists under the table. Instead I stare at his work-worn fingers while he gingerly touches each one of my knuckles.

"You need to pad your hands when you hit that punching bag."

I look at my knuckles, they are pink and raw, a few scabbed wounds that bleed when I use my hands.

"I know." Now I push my plate away. "I'll walk home."

The storm left two feet of new snow beneath a bright sun and a bluebird sky. From the sidewalk in front of my house I reach down and grab a fistful of snow—the whiteness is light and fluffy, slowly melting against the red cotton of my glove. I lie down in the snow and stare up at the sky until a chill takes over my body and forces stiff shakes through my limbs and teeth. I go inside, put on a pot of water for coffee, and go back to that memory, my sister, the last time I saw her face, how she had taken my hand and led me from the bathroom sink to the couch. She insisted I sit so she could snuggle in close to me. I looked at each child, their faces tilted upward, eyes glued to the cartoon on the screen, giggles escaping their mouths from time to time, and I wondered what they remembered. I wondered if they remembered the day I left them. I wondered if she remembered begging me to take her with me. I wondered if any of them would ask me questions about anything. But no one said a word until the cartoon ended, and even then their words were limited to "guess what's" broken up by playful wrestling matches or other forms of showing off. I looked at each one of my little brothers, acutely aware of our separation, the distance that had built up between us, a lonely space that, in that moment, I could make disappear by telling them I'd come back to stay. The words never came out. I didn't even try to form them. I could have forced myself to return to that house, but I knew I wouldn't. I wept, and the kids got calm and looked from me to each other. Noah said, "Don't cry," and Samantha reached up to wipe away my tears. "Okay, okay," I said, and forced myself to smile. "Should we get another cupcake?"

Jonah knocks on my front door, and I, from the window, carefully peer through the blinds at his body. It seems stronger than when I look at him up close. I know there is still that longing in his eyes, that searching look that makes me uncomfortable, but now, from a distance, I see only his frame, a body, strong and calm. I'd answer the door, but I know if I do he'll stay, and we both need him to go away. He sets a package in front of my door and then walks back to his car. I feel relief and a small pang of sadness that I don't recognize as he drives away. I stare at the silver spot of machine that hides his body until there is nothing left to see, but I keep staring into the cold distance, hoping that some kind of warmth will come across the empty space, that his breath will touch my lips, and, for the first time, I'll be happy to feel its warmth. But there's nothing. Nothing except for the small package he had carefully left at the front of my door, inside which, the smell of new leather seeps from a pair of boxing gloves, patiently waiting to protect the exposed knuckles that I strike, again and again, against the punching bag, hoping the broken skin might bring more than the thin layer of blood escaping over my fists.

Breaking

One of the things Jonah especially disliked about me, or at least what I did, was that I fell in love with the Colorado River and became a river runner very early in my twenties. I traded in pointe shoes for cam straps, bowlines, and boats. I commuted from Salt Lake City to Marble Canyon, Arizona, every summer, leaving behind the university, the city's inversion and surrounding mountains for red desert dirt, cliffs, and the Colorado River cooled only by man's construction, the Glen Canyon dam. I'd gotten the job by luck, by knowing someone who worked there, and for many years it grounded me, especially the physicality of it, and the people like Joel, who became a friend and taught me how to read water and drive an S-rig. We are one year and six months apart to the day. I was twenty-one when we met, twenty-two when we did our first trip through the Grand together, and he let me drive my first rapid—Ruby. I caught the eddy on the left and spun the boat out. It was a bad run. He had been quick to blame himself though it had been my fault.

At twenty-six, when I gazed horrified at the positive sign, it was Joel who came to stand next to me when I called him back to the guest bathroom. I was staying at his house—newly purchased by him and his wife. He said, "Take another, the first one is always wrong." I took two more and still the plus sign showed up in blue and I was pissed. Arizona is one of those fucked up states with waiting periods and few clinics that provide abortions. So I called Jonah, who I had not seen in six weeks, to tell him what had happened, and then I went back to work on the river while waiting for my appointment.

On the back of the boat Joel offered me a drink, but I felt guilty even though I knew I would terminate. He'd sensed my discomfort, pushed the drink toward me and said, "It's okay, you're drinking for two now." I laughed, then cried, and he hugged me and said, "At least now we know why you've been such a bitch lately." I laugh-cried and he squeezed me tighter.

Like many women, I now know what it means to be laid back and spread open because my body has become like soil for planting. And when the doctor removed the smallest of growths, it contracted my insides, painfully. And when the nurse told me to stop tensing so much, her voice harsh, her concern that I would bleed more, I relaxed my thighs like an obedient child and felt my eyes burn.

It had been July hot in Phoenix. There were girls lined up in chairs against the walls. Some with lovers, mothers, or alone. I was not alone. I had told my summer-time boss, April, what I had to do, and she was firm about driving me the two hours to the closest abortion clinic and sitting with me in the waiting room. On the drive back to Flagstaff she gave me soup and a book she thought I might like. I laid the book across my knees, sipped on chicken broth, and told her that before the procedure began, the nurse asked if I wanted to hear the heartbeat. "Why would she do that?" April simply nodded her head, a pained look on her face.

I flew back to my winter home, Salt Lake, to rest for a week—April had insisted. I took a cab from the airport to my apartment, which was dense with valley heat, and dragged my mattress to the living room where the air conditioning worked best—the artificial breeze cool against my body. I watched the cottonwoods out the window, the sky a brilliant blue, and my heart beat slow, steady. I was aware of every thump, listening intently for the sound. Jonah came by after work, lay next to me, meaning to ask if I were okay, but his dick was hard, and I had to tell him I couldn't, even though I was trying to show that everything was fine. "Sex," I said, "will give me an infection." And worse, I thought, it would make me want to die. But then I used my hands to try and show everything was alright because I didn't know how to show it wasn't. Afterwards, I wrapped up in a sheet to hide my insides shedding something like coffee grounds, like blood. A few months later I tried to leave him, and that's when I realized that leaving didn't come easy to me.

I have no regrets and I do not wonder about what might have been. But I do feel sadness the way any woman might when her body is opened up and something is pulled out, or opened up and something is shoved in. But we can't even be left alone with our sadness if that's what we choose—our bodies always the topic of some man's debate, internal or otherwise, asking questions like, "Why was she dressed to make a man want to take her down?" I remember what I had been wearing—a red tank top, a flowing skirt I loved, and flip-flops. I do not remember his name because I taught myself not to, though we spent an entire semester in the same political science class. After he finished, I ran out of his apartment and down the street, 900 East in downtown Salt Lake City. Years later and I still avoid that street.

Campus administrators may as well just come out and say women should work harder at not being assaulted; after all, rape just isn't the kind of epidemic bad enough to make real change. So we are left with the Clery Act Reports twisted into unnecessary, violating details of vaginal penetration with fingers, dicks, and whatever the hell. And just to be sure the shame seeps into female bones, the truth about the assaulted woman's sobriety finds its way into the report. After all, if she weren't irresponsible, she wouldn't be such an invitation to men. If I believed such things, I'd say that of myself—I was an irresponsible invitation. That is, I had been drunk. Afterwards, I never said a word, not even when the man whose name I don't remember left wilted flowers that reminded me of his weeping on my doorstep. Whether a woman is wept upon or beaten while being raped, she will carry her scars and an understanding that for the most part, justice is just a dream.

What women do with their own bodies is more than a point of focus for so many, it is an obsession, a fixation, and I do not understand it. Nor do I understand the way brothers become men who make laws and speeches about what can be done with women's flesh, while mothers' soft voices whisper in daughters' ears about modesty until girls understand that it's just another word for shame. Sadly, I think there will always be at least one man holding a Bible on the senate floor shaking his righteousness against us. And there will always be a man begging for relief because he can't penetrate his hurt girlfriend. Always some men will be on women's bodies.

It was Joel who walked up a rough trail in flip-flops and then over the cliffside onto the Talus, his feet taking a beating in the hot rocks and dirt. He approached me carefully. "Rachel, I'm here," he said, and walked toward the body of a woman who had fallen off the cliff. I had seen her fall and die and I could not help though I sat with her and spoke anyway. I'd laid gauze on her wounds to keep the bugs away, waving them off when they had still landed. That morning at breakfast she had talked about how much she loved the blueberry pancakes Joel and I had made, and on the trail, she told me of the thirty years she'd spent hiking Colorado. I had told her I was moving to Missouri and that I was scared to leave the West, and she'd said the mountains would wait for me, to be tough because school could only last so long. And she was tough, and stubborn too. She would not take my hand when I offered it, would not let me help her as we walked near the cliff's edge, and when she fell, she had said nothing, but her friend had screamed. I ran after the body, knowing it was too late and that's all she would be now. But she was still around, her life there in the afternoon heat. I'd spoken to her, repeated "I am so sorry."

I'd muttered those same words the first time I saw death. I was a kid riding in the back seat of my father's car he called Old Girl. He'd given my two older brothers and me ice-cream cones and drove us along Texas back roads. There, ranchers hang coyote skins on fence posts—and I'd mourned their fleshless hides and the cruelty of the hands that ripped fur from flesh. I swear there were catfish heads drying out there too, but I couldn't say why.

In my tenth year as a river runner, I drove away from Missouri, Kansas, Oklahoma, and through Dalhart, Texas, on my way to Arizona. I thought the dirt wasn't good for much but leading into New Mexico dust. The way it coated a dead coyote lying in the median, blowing against painted pictographs on abandoned buildings that once advertised "Authentic Indian Jewelry," made something twist in my stomach, guilt, a pressure on my chest. In the Canyon I'd seen a litter of coyotes running alongside the riverbank, the runt struggling to keep up amidst invasive cheatgrass and tamarisk. I'd slowed my oars, watched their bodies disappear into a den, knowing that because of me, their mamma would have to move them once more. Later, another guide and I pulled boats out of the Colorado and then hopped in the winch truck, rusted and hot, and headed to Meadview, Arizona—trailers upon trailers. We saw a coyote on the road, and he'd swerved to hit her. Pitifully I cried out, reaching for the wheel. He'd firmly responded to my pleas by exclaiming the coyote was nothing but a scavenger, though he'd steered away all the same. I'd leaned back against the sun-soaked leather, cracked and peeling, and thought about how we are all scavengers—people living off a dying river, prosperous Western cities draining the land of her resources, farmers farming where they shouldn't, ranchers grazing their livestock where there shouldn't be any livestock, and us driving past poverty-stricken land with our judgments.

Once, four or five years into my river running career, I stood on the bow of a man's boat to look at the body of a mountain lion that had pulled herself to shore by her own massive paws, or maybe she was washed there by the river—I didn't have the facts. Her perfect golden body sun beat and still, made me feel sick—all her grandness gone and me working with tourists to make a living in her wild. The boatman, mean as he was, looked pained, couldn't stand the sight of a dead thing. I gazed at her carcass spread on a bit of earthen ground amidst the black and pink rocks—Vishnu Schist and Zoroaster Granite. Later I recalled the mountain lion and somehow that recollection felt less like death than sipping coffee on my porch in Missouri, slapping mosquitoes and wishing for Redwall Cliffs and the sound of oars pushing water. And what did that make me? Knowing the bad that'd been done to the wild and me still wishing to go back there, to take from her, to feel alive. All that wishing is like a festering wound, like unnaturally chilled waves lapping at breaking beaches in the Canyon.

Lies

Because I wear down easily, because I get lonely, because I don't know how to leave and stay gone, I go through many break-ups with Jonah. I think I'm supposed to be happy, to get happy with him because he says he has so much love to give me. But I cannot, not fully, because I don't feel it, not the way he does, which he does not seem to mind. Sometimes this makes me even more lonely, sometimes angry. Often I am mean.

At dinner in downtown Salt Lake City the table in the Chinese restaurant is set with paper placemats decorated with Zodiac signs. Jonah and I are both happy for the colorful distraction and read about how he is the Cock, and I am the Dog. We learn that, though we are not warned about one another, we are not recommended for each other either. The dim light over our table covers his displeasure with the menu, which as he points out, has no goddamn beer. I offer him some of my hot tea, but he ignores me, looks back at the placemat and reads aloud the Zodiac recommended matches for the Cock.

Sometimes when we have dinner at the apartment, which we will share for nearly a year, I take bloody flesh out of white packaging paper and carry it to the fire, watch flames rise out of the grill, and wait for coals to glow the perfect temperature.

Sometimes we fight about the cooking, always we fight about the cleaning. And I do not know how to fight right and words that don't seem all that hurtful to me because of where I come from, what I'm used to, are cruel to Jonah. When I say I'm not happy with his dropping out of college or that he lets his parents pay for some of his bills, I say it in the meanest way possible. But instead of grabbing me as my father would have—his thick hands twisting my arms into bruises, his eyes fixed on mine, waiting to draw tears that would not come, Jonah stays gentle. And this withholding of violence means something to me.

During the summer of the year that we live together I work in Arizona as always, and when I return to Salt Lake after months of running trips in the Canyon, I find bags of trash lining a wall in the kitchen, beer cans litter the floor, pizza boxes are piled in stacks on top of the stove, and the sink and countertops are covered with dirty dishes. Gnats crawl and hover over everything, and the once-white wall is now covered in moving black spots. I think Jonah may be punishing me for working out of town so much because I can't believe anyone would purposely live like this, be this lazy. The stench is unbearable, a gnat lands in my eye, another goes up my nose as I take loads of trash out to the dumpster. By the time he walks through the door from work the house is clean. "The place looks nice," he says, reaching for my body, leaning in for a kiss, as his hands slide underneath my shirt where my belly has stayed pale, hidden from Arizona's rays. I wonder if his lip were busted if he would keep his mouth to himself.

In the morning we go to breakfast. Jonah orders French toast and bacon and I order hashbrowns and eggs. He looks at me for a moment. He's hungover and his eyes are not so beautiful when dull, and I wish there were a morning paper to read. He is determined to eat slowly, savoring each bite as he begins, "I can't think of a fucking thing to say to you."

His words stay with me though I don't feel altogether fazed by them, but for some reason they make me think of my father. I find myself recalling how my father tried to steal my education, said it was for my own good—to protect me from the world. He'd given me a heart necklace over a slice of pizza on my thirteenth birthday, said it was a symbol of the beating organ inside me, his property, until he chose to give it to another man. I look up and see Jonah watching me in that old, all-too-familiar way. I'd like to think that his pleading blue eyes might do something to me, might make my heart skip, might make me feel more love, the right kind of love, but they don't. I place my hand over the skin and bones that cover my heart, feel it work to pump blood through my body and I know it beats because it can, and it beats for me, not for this man who I'm finally realizing loves an idea of who he thinks I might be. And I realize that I mainly love the idea of who I think he might be, too. But even so, even when I look back now and know how impossible it was for me to be with anyone in a healthy way at that point in my life, I like to think that there had been something real between us.

Ways of Leaving

The story goes like this: a Utah writer came home early and found a man in bed with his wife. In a fit of rage, the writer took the man to the Salt Lake City Avenues cemetery and forced him to sit on the frozen ground of January. And while he sat there trembling with cold, the writer stood above him, smoked an entire pack of cigarettes, and flicked each still-smoking butt at the stunned lover. Then he just walked away. I used to live in the Avenues and have walked through that cemetery many times myself; it's a bit of a climb underneath that unmistakable western sky, pierced by tips of pines and the occasional Box-elder oak tree. I've also read that writer's stories. The one about the two women who nicked their shared lover's Achilles tendon so he couldn't walk away from them, couldn't leave them, has stayed with me over the years. Probably because I wonder about tactics against leaving, the ways we leave, the ways we lose.

I became close with a man in my MFA program who lived just below that Avenues cemetery. One night he guided me through the headstones. It had been cold, and we climbed to the top of the cemetery and sat on a concrete bench. I'd pressed close for the heat of his body while we looked across the Salt

Lake Valley, city lights for miles and just beyond them, the Wasatch Mountains, beautiful, blue, and snow tipped. "This is why I brought you up here, kind of a nice view—wanted you to see it," he said. I remember briefly thinking it was funny that he thought the view was unknown to me, that this place, my home, was new to me. Then he had nudged my shoulder and I looked at him. He was pointing, not to the valley or the mountains, but at the ground, at a tombstone, across which read "Hanson" in bold letters.

In *One Love Affair*, Jenny Boully writes a list of things that ripen to die, "plums, flesh, girl flesh, love affairs. . . ." I sometimes think of the way my relationships have ended—how by the end there must have been moments when we looked at one another and saw rot. It's not the most painful thing, but it stings a little still. Though really it's the memories triggered by a touch or sighting, usually brief and seemingly unrelated to my past, that wrench my insides and make me recall things I'd rather forget. Like when my little brother asked me to teach him to read and I didn't. Or when a friend died in an accident and all I could think of was the last time I saw him—how I'd refused to hug and make up after a stupid fight. Or the way I tried to save an animal—stayed up all night outside on my parents' porch holding the puppy. I tried to get her to take food and water and held her close. When I look back at my child-self sitting in the humid dark of Tennessee holding that small thing in my own small hands, I see just how alone the two of us were that night, and still I can't help but think how I should have done more to save her.

When I was four years old, Addie, the mother who lived in the house behind mine, reached over the chain-link fence that separated her backyard from ours and gave me an apple. She told me to stop drinking the pickle juice I'd taken from my parents' refrigerator because it was bad for me. I obeyed though I told her I didn't like apple peels and she told me to eat it anyway. Addie was married to the preacher who abused the family dog, who beat his son for looking at the stiches on my forehead when we were all supposed to be napping. As a kid I hadn't wondered where Addie was when the beating went on, but now I do. I think a lot of bad must have been happening in that house, and I suppose that's obvious because one day Addie put herself in her garage, closed the door, started the car, and sat breathing in what she must have thought of as merciful fumes. Only part of her died though, so in the end there had been no mercy and her death turned out to be slow. The fumes had damaged her brain, but her husband found her before they took all of her. He ended up putting her in some kind of a "home." I never saw her again after that day she went into the garage, but my mother did. She said Addie wasn't Addie anymore. At some point I started wondering if her body had still been enough Addie to know to tense when her husband walked through her doorway.

Boully also writes a list of "things that bruise"—they are much like the "list of things that ripen to die." Fruit and flesh and a place to put the name of a man. She writes: "[his name here]" at the bottom of both lists. The generality of it surprised me the first time I read that list, but then felt love: love given when it should be withheld, or love withheld when it should have been given, has a way of bruising. There is almost always a way of being bruised or making bruises.

The same man who took me to the cemetery used to keep dinner for me until I was out of my late-night class. It would be near ten o' clock and I'd take in the star-filled night, breathe in the cold air, and feel happy thinking of him. It was the little things he did that both surprised and gave me joy. Like when I spent hours in the library staring at my computer screen covered with my words, strung out vague thoughts and incomplete sentences, and my eyes would burn. I'd lean back and look out the windows toward the mountains and feel sad I'd neglected them so much for my studies. Then I'd close my eyes and push my knuckles into them, rubbing unmercifully. He had found me like this, sat down across from me, piling his books on the table, and then got up and left. I'd imagined he'd gone for coffee, but when he returned, he'd pulled a small bottle of eye drops from his pocket and sat them in front of me without saying a word. I think that's when it first occurred to me that I loved him.

Love is odd, especially the varying pace of it. Sometimes I think of what could ever have made Addie love her preacher husband. I suspect he hid his cruelty at first, maybe it had surprised her, and maybe she thought it would leave with the arrival of their children. I remember seeing her, months before she tried to commit suicide, lying in her living room. It was like her whole house had been stilled out of fear, and it felt like we were all laid out, fragile. She was babysitting me, and I was supposed to be napping. But I peeked through the den door and saw her across the way, lying on the sofa. A yellow blanket with tiny rosebuds speckled across it was spread underneath her thin body. Her ankles were pale, her toenails a deep red, her hair a bright red. She lay there staring at the ceiling, her chest moving up and down, slow, long exhales and inhales. I saw her husband walk in and lay himself on top of her, but she hadn't moved except to catch her breath and hold it. I scooted back onto my pallet and hid beneath the blankets.

Once I picked up a bottle of chocolate syrup and held it up to the man who used to bring me eye drops, right there amid marshmallow cream and candy toppings. I said, "I think this and some vanilla ice cream were the only sweet things I had for an entire summer when I was like eleven or twelve. Back then it came in cans, not this plastic bottle. My brother brought it home along with a package of mushroom fettuccini pasta. I don't know where he got it, or maybe my parents left it for us, I can't recall. We had been so excited to have something besides popcorn to eat, but that didn't keep us from trying to out-gross the other at the table with mouthfuls of creamy pasta. We were pretty nasty kids." I laughed. And he said, "When you laugh after telling me things like that, it makes me want to cry." I wanted to laugh again, to do something that would end this moment I had no idea what to do with. Instead I had just fallen silent and placed the syrup back on the shelf.

One night after having sex, the man who got sad when I spoke of my childhood revealed that after an argument we'd had, he'd reconnected with an ex-girlfriend. They had planned a vacation together. Though we had made up, he was not going to cancel the trip. I sat up in his bed and pulled the sheets around my naked body, trying to find words, to form a response to his words, but I was speechless. I said nothing, but in the darkness

I got myself out of his bed, reached for my clothes and began to put them on. He turned the light on before I was able to dress under the cover of shadows and it glared at my body, made me feel translucent, and I wanted him to turn it back off, wanted him to turn away from my nakedness, but he watched me closely, already knowing too much of me. I felt soft, overripe, trying hard to stiffen my bruised insides.

I took my ripe wounds and drove to the top of the foothills, just above that cemetery and sat looking out across the valley. It had been dark and ethereal—perfect. I found myself staring at the headstones, the dark iron fence, the cold grass, the black desert sky consumed with perfect stars that remind me of the time I first realized there was no god, and seeing a falling star, wondered if believers thought them a sign of the fallen, the faithless. I had been sixteen when that realization came to me and it had made me laugh low and soft, knowing my mother was beneath an icon of Christ burning herself with cigarettes, wounds she would make me see, faulting me for not stopping her from killing her own flesh.

I wonder about my own way of leaving, the way I always stay too long. And I wonder about Addie. *Did she try to leave before trying to kill herself?* I wonder if she was one of those women who planned her escape over and over in her mind, but never did make a move, because where would she go? Or maybe she had made a move and her preacher husband had found her, had done something terrible to make her go back. I wonder if, like in that Utah writer's story, she felt cut up, bound to a man she could not walk away from, and he'd done that to her, made sure to keep her from leaving. But she went on ahead and found a way—not the best way, not a complete way—but a way to show that if she didn't feel like she could leave, she could at least show she wanted to.

Sunnyside

In the first few years after I finally found my way of leaving, of running away from home, after I turned eighteen and it was safe for me, I tried to find ways to stay connected to my little sister and brothers. I wrote them letters that they never received, placed phone calls to disconnected phone lines, and tried to keep track of all the places my parents moved to, but in six years I had no luck.

One hot August afternoon when I was twenty-three, I went whipping through red traffic lights and would have kept on going but for encountering traffic at a standstill at the corner of 1500 East a few blocks below Sunnyside Drive in Salt Lake City. The brakes of my little car have stopped working, or so I think, but in reality, I probably hadn't noticed them getting softer and softer over time.

I pump the brakes over and over before bracing myself for impact with the Hummer in front of me. When I hit I'm surprised it doesn't hurt worse, though the front end of my car is demolished. I'm only a little dazed when I notice the old man of the Hummer hobbling over to my car. He looks pissed, which prompts me to reach into the glove compartment for my insurance information.

"I've called the cops," he says, before I even get out of the car.

"Okay. I'm really sorry, I just lost my brakes at the top of the hill," I say.

"Sure you did," the old man says.

Fucker, I think as I push my driver-side door open and walk to curb, light a cigarette, and wait for the cop to arrive. As I sit there, I look past the smoking hood of my 1990 Honda Accord, its gray paint peppered with spots of rust, and toward the cottonwoods. I spent a lot of time up in those canyons a few weeks after arriving to Utah. I'd met a cocky boy I didn't think much of who lived across the street from me, but when he offered to take me rock climbing with his friends, I gave him a second chance. I liked him better in the mountains; he was calmer, kinder, and taught me how to climb and snowboard. But in the valley, he was different and used to shake me awake, complaining about my sweaty fits of fearful speak and tears.

"Why are you so emotional?" he'd said.

We hadn't lasted long, though for a bit of time the sweat-induced dreams became less frequent. When they picked up again, though, I would sometimes jolt upright in the stillness of my small apartment, the image of Luke frowning as I walked away from him. I remember Luke waking me up nearly every morning, lying next to me, his thumb in his mouth, his huge eyes patient, his small fingers tickling my earlobe until I opened my eyes. Sometimes I lay there with eyes closed, not ready to wake up and get going. When I finally did open my eyes, though, he would smile, thumb still inside his mouth. I loved all my little siblings the same but was closest to Luke, and from the time he was able to walk he'd come to me during the night, crying until I lifted him up and tucked him in safe. Once when he was a little bigger and could pull himself up on his own, I locked my bedroom door to discourage him. I wanted a night free of kicks and a morning where I didn't wake up to wet sheets. He beat on my door and cried, and I ignored him, hoping he'd give up and go back to his bed. He didn't, and finally I gave in. And later, in the wee hours of the morning I woke to a cold, wet, and apologetic baby. He was my sweet baby, but always I'll remember the time I locked him out and will cringe with guilt.

Days before this car accident I'd finished another river season in the Grand Canyon. I came back to Utah, moved into a new apartment in Salt Lake City, and having graduated in the spring, was wondering what I was going to do with myself. All that year I'd planned on law school, on doing something that could make money because somewhere in the back of my mind I thought if I had money, I'd have a way to get the babies. But I was not law school material—I couldn't even make it through the LSAT—I blacked out at the beginning of the test. Something like anxiety, something like a fog, a haze all around me, and then my head was on the desk, and when I came to, time was up. I'd answered exactly one question.

There were times in the comfort of my own space when I'd feel grounded, unmovable on the floor; though never regretting my choice to run away, I was desperate to forget the loss that came with that decision. I'd comforted myself by thinking if I worked hard enough, I could eventually fix things with my siblings, but the belief had wavered. The weight of this realization felt like sick failure.

Back on the curb of Sunnyside Avenue the old man drives away in his car, a tow truck arrives for mine, and the cop nears me, so I stand.

"If you were my daughter, I'd tell you not to bother fixing the car. Your money would be better spent on a new one," the cop says.

"Okay," I say, knowing I've no money for another car, but still finding myself curious about how easy those fatherly words were for him to utter.

I think of my own father—he wouldn't have done much except maybe make a crack about *women* drivers, followed by his insistence that he should have known better than to let me behind the wheel. My father never would teach me anything about cars—only the boys needed such knowledge. I'd resented that, and after I left home and had a car of my own, I'd bought a manual and tools, determined to teach myself what I could. Just a few weeks before I'd replaced my alternator and it occurs to me now that maybe, just maybe, I fucked something up and that's why my car is crushed and smoking and being towed to a junk yard. I keep the thought to myself.

"It looks like your master cylinder went out, that's why you lost your brakes," the cop says, as he hands me a ticket.

"Oh, okay," I say.

"It's pretty hot out here, do you want a ride home?" he asks.

"That's okay, I'm used to the heat, thanks though."

He shrugs his shoulders and returns to his car, and the tow truck pulls my broken car farther down Sunnyside Avenue and out of view. I stand there for a while, stuck on the thought of my father. Of all the people in my life, I can't make sense of him. As a kid I'd certainly tried, had always secretly hoped that he would leave my mother and take all us kids away with him. I had this crazy dream that he would figure it out, that he would see all he had to do was leave my mother and then we could be safer, happier, could go to school and just be normal. But he never could bring himself to do that; I guess that's why he had affairs, his own escape of sorts. It bothers me a lot, not the cheating so much, who could blame him for that, but his unwillingness to give his kids the best chance at a good life. What did his staying accomplish for anyone? I guess when I get right down to it, my father is a fucked-up enabler to my mother, and that makes him worse than her because he let her get away with all her bullshit, helped her hurt us. That's a hard thing to wrap my head around—him being worse than her—because between the two of them, he had always been the kindest.

I make myself stop thinking of my father and instead begin wondering what I'm going to do without my car, when my cell phone rings. As with all numbers I don't recognize, I answer the call because there is always the chance one of my letters made it to my siblings and maybe one of them is calling me. I guess a letter did get through, because when I answer it's my mother's voice on the other end.

"Rachel, it's your mother."

"Where are you?" I ask, and quickly start walking home.

"You don't need to worry about that," my mother responds.

Already I know how this conversation is going to play out, already I know she's bored, and she wants to toy with me. Already I know my mother plays to hurt.

"Put the babies on, let me talk to them!" I say.

"Rachel," a sigh, slight pause, "They don't want to talk to you. And your father and I don't want you talking to them until you get your heart right with us and God."

By now I'm nearing my apartment, and all the bustling in my neighborhood, the heat of a desert sun, and the sound of traffic—all those things I usually notice suddenly dim in the harsh reality that my mother's voice triggers. I barely realize I'm inside my apartment when I say, "Just put Samantha on."

And for the briefest moment, she does. I hear Samantha's voice, more grown up but still such a little seven-year-old voice say, "Rachie?"

"Samantha! How are you?"

"I'm okay."

"Do you remember me?"

"Yes." She begins to cry, and I try not to.

"We need to talk," my mother says, taking the phone from my sister.

"Not yet." I tell her, "Let me talk to the boys first."

"I've told you no. I shouldn't have let you talk to Samantha. If you want to talk to the children, then you are going to have to get your life back on track," my mother insists.

My head starts to ache, my stomach in knots, and I chew on my lip until I can taste my blood. I remain silent for a few moments, contemplating what to do next. The longer I say nothing, the more the rage takes over my body because I know I will never be able to make her happy, not even enough to let me talk to my brothers and sister. I'm frozen in place, still but for the quick beats of my heart. Finally, I take a breath, exhale, then ask my mother why she is such an evil bitch. She tells me I blew it, that I have no one but myself to blame, and then she hangs up. I set the phone on the floor and lie down next to it. Sweat forms beads on my face and chest. I can feel my skin sticking to the old wooden boards of my living room as I lie there and let the memories sweep over me, full force and clear as day.

I remember my little brothers asking for pizza and me feeding them peanut butter and jelly, oatmeal, or Tater Tots. Sometimes I made spaghetti. I remember fucking up a Christmas when I took the little money I had somehow managed to save and, instead of spending it all on my siblings, bought trinkets for my ballet teacher's kids because all the other ballet students gave her family gifts, and, after all, she didn't make my parents pay for my classes, didn't let them use money as an excuse to keep me out of the studio. So I bought the trinkets and then spent the rest on toys for my brothers, toys that, as it would turn out, break after an hour of play. I remember Ben driving me around that night even though he couldn't legally drive. It was close to Christmas, and I must have been thirteen and hoped like crazy that my parents were lying about not celebrating Christmas again this year. Ben helped pay for the toys, too. We both felt badly for our little brothers because even though they knew not to believe in Christmas miracles, they did. And always there was none.

I remember Logan, my first baby brother, in a sleeper with dark eyes, dimples, very pink tongue, lots of crying, lots of smiles. He was not closest to me, but to my oldest brother who walked the halls with him more than I did, who tended him the most, at least for the first few years of his life. I remember being ten years old and dressing Logan up in my old clothes and telling the neighbors he was a girl, and he just laughed and laughed, his white-blond curls a mess. I remember the times I failed to be better, to be the best. I remember my baby brother growing and parting his now brown hair, putting on his best blue jeans, a blue or red shirt, white socks, and waiting for something to do, for somewhere to go. But there is nowhere, and he's tending his appearance for nothing. And I, a big sister, see and it makes me tired.

I remember a baby with yellow hair. A baby who had the sweetest temperament. My fourth baby brother—little, accident prone Michael. His poor face would get a black eye from a toy flung across the room by one of his brothers, catching it right in the face. And just as the black and purple gave way to a yellow healing green, another bruise would take place. Michael cried when he hurt, but so often found something to laugh about before the tears had dried. And I became a gone sister, who would never be able make up for it all.

I remember when Noah was born, I was the first person aside from my parents to hold him. My father insisted I do so, afraid that, like when Logan was born, I'd be disappointed I didn't get a sister. I didn't mind by then though, and I held Noah, happy to be the first sibling to hold him. I remember him stretched out in red sleepers. And when he grew, grew on his own, always a little on his own. Maybe I did not squish him enough, maybe he did not want it, but I remember times when he'd snuggle in close, looking at pictures in the book I read to him and the rest of the babies. I remember so clearly how it felt when he pressed close trying to get warm, his feet jutting just over the edge of the couch cushion. And I remember his rage when I yelled at him to pick up his toys or when I put him to bed too early because I was tired, because I wanted a break. Sometimes I was a real shit sister.

I lie on my floor remembering. I remember and remember long into the darkness, pressing my body heavy into the ground, as if I could somehow tempt it to spread apart and take me inside.

Writing You

I'm still in the West but before long will be moving to Missouri to earn a PhD. Being a river runner hasn't yet become bittersweet, and I haven't yet started moving around from one academic job to another. I'm nearing thirty years old and trying to write the story of my childhood in the South but I don't. I don't feel like it and the night is too enticing. The air perfect, clear, and void of any hint of the inversion that usually plagues the valley in winter. January has passed, and February is slipping away too, offering a break from the thick haze that has hung over Salt Lake City. So I go for a walk up A Street to 7th Avenue, then down to City Creek Canyon. The creek bed, mostly dry in the winter, makes me think of water in Arizona, of how the Paria could be so near dry for weeks and then flash hard, pushing sediment into the Colorado River. The Paria still runs wild, though, not like little dammed up City Creek, though it flashes sometimes too. I hadn't seen it, but heard of the years it flooded State Street, the aftermath leaving downtown Salt Lake looking less pristine, more like regular cities, not so clean-cut.

I come out at the base of City Creek Canyon, walk past historic houses to South Temple Street where I pause, take in this weird town that has become my home, then head back to my apartment. Once there, I kick off my snow boots and try to shake off the cold. In the kitchen I stare into the refrigerator aimlessly before deciding to pour a glass of wine from an open bottle. I take the wine to the bathroom where I run a hot bath. The water makes my cold toes tingle, bubbles come all the way up to my chin, and the wine, mixed with heat, gives me a buzz. I'm tired but happy in my own bathtub, in my own little apartment where the warm water is also my own. My eyes close and go straight to little girl me. I remember when I was ten years old, in the bathtub, cold and exhausted. A body that was not its own. I had tried to forget about child me for a long time because it is all too messy. But the memories insisted, and the words had started to come.

I keep my eyes closed as the water cools and try not to let my story overwhelm me. But then I am her again, and my mother is there hovering over me, scanning my naked body. She detests it. My grown woman's body, and I feel her stare as I had many times as a child, a teenager, a person who for so long was not her own. I sit up quickly then, water splashing to the floor as I pull the plug.

I think about the river while my wet hair drips over my shoulders. And I think about the bluebird sky, the hot sun reflecting off fresh snow in the cottonwoods and the sound my snowboard makes on the mountain. When on the mountain or the water, I always forget about my mother, the haze of the South, that desperate prick of hopelessness. It is the stillness where she catches up with me, where my little brothers and sister catch up with me, too. I don't know them, they don't know me, and in my absence, I know she taught them how to hate me.

I pace in my apartment now. I think of Noah, the one sibling I'd been able to get in touch with in the last few months. It had taken some digging to find him, phone calls to Orthodox churches in towns where I'd learned my parents might have been. Mostly priests were willing to talk to me, and the ones that knew my parents at one point or another always asked if I was okay. One priest wanted to send me his book on sacrifice, another extended an invitation to visit, and all of them ended the phone call with a blessing that I'd accepted out of politeness.

My chest hurts for Noah, for the baby that he was, and the hardened young man he has become. When he turned eighteen years old, he didn't come to me like I had always imagined he would, like I imagined all of my younger siblings would. He waited nearly a year to call. He let my letters go unanswered. He was so angry with me. So angry that I had left him, and I can't blame him. I am angry too.

When he calls again, I answer, hear his grown-up voice and wait for more of his angry spews to shoot into that place in my stomach where everything hurts so bad it makes me sick. But tonight it doesn't happen. Tonight he asks, "Do you remember I used to call you Rachie?" I see his face, that beautiful boy who was already tired, and simply say "Yes, I remember."

Epilogue

In my dream, I am in a house that is not mine, not my family's either. I am grown, not the me I am now, and not entirely the girl who ran away from home as a teenager. In the dream world, I still know my siblings. In the dream world, they are still mine and I am theirs. In this dream world, I am sad, and they are children aware of sadness but not sure why it permeates their lives.

I'm standing at the top of an outdoor set of stairs that lead from a large back porch down to a boat dock. The water is deep, and it is dark, and it has that lake smell that emerges from stagnant water. The water is cold, and I have no intention of getting in. I'm wearing sneakers, the kind of tank top my mother would not have allowed me to wear. I have jeans—they are baggy, but not too baggy, my mother would have begrudgingly approved these. My little brother Luke, who is always the one who comes to me in my dreams for as long as I can remember since leaving home, is a little older than he was when I left him behind. He rushes past me, his fine brown hair cut tight to his head, and he has on only shorts, and what seems like a diaper underneath, the top of which sticks out above the waist of his pants. I think, he's too old to be wearing that. *Why is he wearing that?* And then I realize he intends to jump straight down into the water. He's rushing toward it and I am as if someone suddenly awakened, but I cannot speak. I know he can't swim, and I want to call out to him not to jump in, but no words come out, not even a muffled cry. He jumps, laughs as the water swallows him.

I reach the end of the dock, searching the place where he went in, trying to make out the whiteness from the top of his diaper. I see it and him being pushed away from the dock. I dive in after whiteness. On the bottom of the lake, not so deep as I imagined it to be, I find myself right in front of my little brother. The water is trying to pull him further away from shore. I reach for him, feel my fingertips brush against his baby belly, and I curl my fingers around his waist on both sides trying for a grip even as the water works at pulling him from me. I'm terrified to let go and try for a better grip, terrified not to try, but in an instant my brother intertwines his arms around my forearms, his small fingers gripping tightly and I am able to gather him in close to my chest and he moves his arms to my neck and holds on with all the will his tiny body can muster. I push off the lake bottom, kicking my feet, freeing one arm from my brother to help swim us up to the top. Back on the dock, I'm weakened and, on my knees, and he stands, drenched, and I am drenched, and he does not loosen his arms wrapped so tightly around my neck. I hold onto him, and my body begins to shake. I feel a pang of emptiness that he should fill because he is not lost, he is right there in front of me so everything must be okay, but it's not and I don't know why.

That's the moment I wake up. I gasp, sit up so fast I knock my cat, Fairbanks, off the bed. My partner reaches out and puts his hand on my back.

"What is it?" he asks.

"I dreamt about my little brother. It was not good."

He asks if I want to talk about it, but I don't. I lie back down and wonder about my brother now. He's twenty-six. Does he know how to read? Does he work? Does he have someone to love?

I notice how my body hurts. I must have been sleeping hard. When I look at my skin in the early light seeping through our curtains, it's covered in red impressions—looks as if I slept on uneven ground. My other cat, Seymour, picks a fight with my partner's Punchy. We've all been living together since December, and though our three cats in total are not, by any means, angels, the screaming hisses surprise us both. I hush all three of them and they move to their respective corners, until Punchy crawls under the bed and comes out on my side of the floor, lies on her back and cries at me as she does when she wants food. Sometimes I think the three of them play at fighting to trick me out of bed for an earlier breakfast. I roll over, wait a few minutes so as not to seem to give into her demands. She meows louder. Fairbanks joins in. The dog, Behr, has wakened now, too. My partner moans and tosses back the covers. I follow suit.

All six of us stand in the kitchen now, the animals looking up at us anxiously waiting. My partner and I stand in our underwear, struggling with bowls, dry food, wet food, medicine.

"Does Behr get his pills this morning or was that yesterday?"

"I'll crush Seymour's pill, you do Behr's."

We fall into a rhythm. My partner begins his mealtime monologue: "In the beginning god created dry food, and god looked upon the dry food and saw that it was good. This was the first day."

Then jumping from the Old Testament to the New he continues: "In the time of Caesar Augustus a decree went out that all wet food should be taxed, and so being of the house of Baker Place, Behr and Punchy came to North Carolina from the East, and Seymour who was with the child Fairbanks came from the West, and when they arrived they waited in the kitchen, for there was no room for them in the bed. In the fields the shepherds were watching over their flocks when suddenly an angel appeared in the sky, and said, 'Behold, I bring you good tidings of great wet food. For this very day, in the city of Asheville, wet food is served. And this shall be a sign to you, you will find the wet food in the kitchen and lying in a dish.' Then the angel was joined by a host of angels who sang, 'Glory to wet food in the highest, and peace to wet food on earth.' This was the second day. And on the third day, everyone rested."

The kitchen goes quiet but for the smacking of hungry animals and my low laughter. My partner, who grew up Catholic though is no longer religious, walks to the bathroom, calls out behind him as I begin to make coffee: "That's really blasphemous. Don't put that in one of your essays."

I start the coffee, knowing I'll need a full pot to help me shake the dream, which I fear will be a tough thing to do. I turn my thoughts to writing. Seymour follows me to my study licking his chops, hops up on the desk and begins washing his face. I stare at him, surprised at how well he moves around for a fifteen-year-old cat. He's too skinny, though his coat still has a good sheen to it. The vet tells me he's an old man and that his time is limited. Though I know it's irrational, I hate her for saying such a thing. Still, I watch him close for signs of pain—I will not let him suffer. I can see that this morning is a good morning for him though, and I laugh a little and tell him he is my longest relationship and that he is my best friend. Then I open my laptop, and stare at the screen, the memory of my baby brother pushing so hard on my chest it's as if I had left him only yesterday.

Of all my siblings, I was closest to Luke—I called him Lukey the Love. I remember one time, when Luke must have been about two and I was thirteen, he set my bed on fire. He must have woken up from his nap, found some matches (to this day I don't know where they came from), and climbed back in my bed—his favorite place to sleep, and lit matches and dropped them on top of the comforter until one caught the thing on fire. He screamed, and then my older brother Ben was yelling. I think I was there, I think Ben handed Luke to me, then he put the fire out. It had been small and was put out easily. Ben later mocked Luke because he had just sat there and screamed, not trying to get away from the fire. I remember being angry that Ben made fun of him—he was only a baby. I look back at that and wonder where I'd been because Luke tended to want to be close to me; even if I left one room for another momentarily, he would insist on coming with me more often than not. I wonder if I had snuck off and hidden with a book somewhere, probably exhausted and not wanting to tend to Luke or anyone else. This is a memory I don't like to recall, and though I don't know this for certain, I think that Luke may be doing worse than my other little siblings. Although I know, on an intellectual level at least, that this is not my fault, that part of me that still wakes up in a sweat even after two decades of being gone isn't so sure.

I tell my partner this story, this incomplete memory, one night in the kitchen while I'm sitting on the countertop drinking vodka. I take a sip to keep from tears. He sighs and, knowing how I hate to be hugged when sad, keeps his distance.

"I know I can't change the past, but no matter what I'm going to make sure that you are never forced to take care of anyone you don't choose to care for," he says.

I think about this, take another sip of vodka and nod. We both know I won't let that happen myself, but I'm glad he says this anyway. Something about the not being alone with how the past affects my present is comforting, and it's new. I find myself staring at his tattoos. For a few moments still I fixate on his Fox and the Crow of Aesop fables tattoo. At first it reminded me of when I read that story when I was a kid. I see the pictures in the book so vividly still. The book had been beautiful once, but after eight kids had gotten their hands on it, it was a shameful mess. I hadn't thought about that book, that story even, until my partner got the tattoo. That was last September and now it's May and it occurs to me, as I'm looking at the tattoo, that I'm thinking of my partner as he sat in the tattoo shop, the soft buzz from the tattoo pen in the air, ink and blood. I think about how he loves fables so much he put the image of one on his body. I love that he loves something that much. I love that he loves literature. I realize more and more that, at least when I'm awake, old memories aren't holding me back in the past as easily as they once did, and instead of wanting to punish myself for it as I might have before, somehow I just feel unbelievably relieved.

ACKNOWLEDGMENTS

This was a difficult story to write, and I owe gratitude to countless individuals for their support as I undertook this project. Thank you to Paisley Rekdal, for her patience as I worked at "catching up" while I made a first stab at writing this story many years ago. Thank you to Anand Prahlad for his advocacy, honesty, and encouragement. Thank you to Esther Lee, Danielle Cadena Deulen, Natanya Anne Pulley, and Susan McCarty who read early excerpts of this work with more care than it deserved. Thank you to Colgate University for the gift of time that the Olive B. O'Connor Fellowship provided me. Thank you especially to Jennifer Brice and Peter Balakian. A special thanks to CJ Hauser for their kindness and care, and for enthusiastically being game for a Colorado River trip. Thank you to my river people, of whom there are many.

Thank you, "Scary Larry" Andrews, for being proud of me. Thank you to my CoMo friends, especially Gordon Sauer and Austin Segrest. Thank you to Elizabeth McConaghy for, among many things, helping me off the floor that day in Tate Hall. Thank you to Lena Lander and Chelsea DeWeese for their love and for always rooting for my work. Thank you to the beautiful poet, Diamond Forde, for being a friend and voice of sanity.

Thank you to my North Carolina friends. A massive thank you to the enormously talented writer, Ye Chun, for believing in my work and above all for her friendship. Thank you to the University of South Carolina Press, especially my editor, Aurora Bell, for putting this book out in the world. Finally, thank you to Jonathan Brown for his unbelievable patience, for reading various drafts of this book, and for braving the ups and downs that plagued me as I worked out the right way to tell this story.

Earlier versions of material for several chapters in this book were previously published in the following journals:

"Breaking," *The Iowa Review* (Fall 2016).
"Dislocations," *So to Speak: a feminist journal of language & arts* (Fall 2011).
"Education," *Best of the Net* (2015).
"Education," as "Hunger Fishing," *Juked* (Spring 2017).
"End of Prayer," *South Dakota Review,* 50th anniversary issue (Fall 2013).
"On Seventeen in Appalachia," *Hairstreak Butterfly Review* (Spring 2019).
"Prism," *Creative Nonfiction* (Spring 2013).
"Talking in Tongues," *storySouth* (Spring 2011).
"Ways of Leaving," *American Literary Review* (Spring 2016).